ARTHRITICS
CAN
FIGHT BACK

D0885838

by R.J. Anderson

The authors intent is not to directly or indirectly dispense medical advice or prescribe the use of any product referred to in this book. The intent is to inform those interested that the possibility exists that cultures and science of people not of the United States may have found a product beneficial to arthritics.

The author believes the citizens of The United States have the right to be informed, and the right to decide for themselves the value of a product which has not been found to cause harm to the human organism.

Any product you see fit to use following the information contained in this book is prescribing for yourself, which is your Constitutional right, but the publisher and author assume no responsibility.

A RANDISCO BOOK

Published by Randisco, Inc.
3011 West Palo Verde
Phoenix, Arizona 85017

ISBN: 0-9617798-0-2
Produced and Printed by
Graphics Management, Los Angeles, CA

This book is true to the best of my knowledge and ability, although parts are recited from memory, such as exact words of conversations. Wherever possible those involved have critiqued the book.

A great deal of the book is recorded in court transcripts, official documents, etc., of which I have possession. They are available for scrutiny if desired.

Some of the names have been changed to protect the guilty or innocent as the case may be. We all must live inside our own minds. In most cases, we create through our conscience the very worst possible punishment. God gave us this method so we may rectify mistakes, to clear the conscience, and proceed as a better human being.

I pray that we, all of the human race, would consider the power contained in this human ability to do right by our fellow man, that a better world might follow.

R. J. Anderson

FROM A
DOCTOR'S POINT OF VIEW

R.J. "Dick" Anderson is a 46 year old, very energetic and brilliant man. For twenty years of his life, he suffered the extreme torments of arthritis.

The miracle of "Earth's Magic" is responsible for his present good health.

He has spent the past six years doing in depth research on this herbal compound. He has worked with several prominent rheumatalogists and manufacturing chemists.

In the company of perhaps America's top Chinese herbalist, he made an extensive trip to Hong Kong to learn all he could about the twenty-two herbs in "Earth's Magic".

I was introduced to the product in March 1982. There were many arthritics in my medical practice. I prescribed it extensively for these past four years with uniformly miraculous results.

These patients, almost to a person, claim fantastic relief from the pain and disability from all kinds of arthritis.

The side effects have been nearly non-existent.

In my opinion, the field testing that has been done by Mr. Anderson and myself plus several other prominent rheumatalogists has. produced irrefutable evidence that "Earth's Magic" is a safe and effective remedy for arthritis. None have claimed that it cures the disease but it has given fantastic relief to most.

Sherman W. Meyer, D.O.
Physician & Surgeon

Dr. Meyer is a nationally known physician and surgeon emeritus who has distinguished himself by his extensive efforts in establishing osteopathic hospitals in many states.

Here is what one expert says about R.J. Anderson's efforts.

"The grass roots movement to return to natures way in the control of our lives continues to gain ground. This interesting and exciting book is one man's experiences in his quest to use natures approach to improve mankinds state of health. You will be intrigued by the road blocks that he faces and overcomes. Read the book and decide for yourself!"

QUALITIVITY
Consultants to the Health Care and Consumer Products Industry

Owen B. Lamb, Ph.D.
President

Mr. Lamb spent 20 years of his career with the FDA.

I dedicate this book to everyone I have known in my lifetime, because I have stolen something from each of you. I have looked for your best qualities and taken those for my own use. You have made my life richer, a smile here, encouraging word there, a bit of wisdom.

But especially to those of you from whom I learned the meaning of life and love-Mom & Dad, sisters and brother, wives (yes, all three) Jeanne, Liz, and Louisa. Children Carol, Bill, Mark, Joanne, Susan, Staci, Rob and Rich, I love you all!

But extra especially to
JUDIE
-who understands-

Author's Statement

I have read perhaps 6,000 books in my 46 years. At about twelve years of age, I started with the King James Bible. I was rebellious and refused to accept my parent's faith at face value. I thank my Dad for telling me, "Find your own answer, son, it is here." He then handed me the bible. It took me about four years of arduous labor to get through it; I put it down a thousand times! How upsetting, finding I was thinking like my parents but too stubborn to admit it. I did, however, learn some great truths.

I cannot believe anyone writes for their own pleasure. I have suffered the pang of probable rejection, the loneliness of seclusion from friends and family, the tears of rembrance, the copious amounts of perspiration, and the frequent lack of inspiration and sleep it has required.

I am. a novice who will probably never write again. My hat is off to the professionals, those blessed by God with a gift, you have brought me a world of pleasure and knowledge, Clavell, Michener, Auel, Uris, and on, and on, and on.

A special thanks to God:

''From whence cometh my strength''.

Forward

It is a well known and accepted fact that the human body has the capability to produce disease fighting products. We know it as our immune system. This system can become impaired by any number of factors. One very important factor is to deprive the body of the nutrition it requires to fulfill its potential. For example, a body can become calcium deficient which will, if allowed to continue, have devastating effects on the skeletal structure. To combat this deficiency, any number of foods high in calcium can be eaten which will allow the body to heal itself. The very core of life itself is found in the food chain.

No one diet has ever been known to supply the human body with every nutrient necessary to keep it in utopian condition. Honey, by the way, is the only natural food known to contain all twenty-two of the essential nutrients to maintain life. This does not mean of course that one could live on honey alone, but it does give one an idea of the value of this food.

There exists on the earth several tribes of people who live extremely long and healthy lives. One of these tribes live high in the Himalayan mountains. Death before age 100 is the exception rather than the rule. Many live far beyond this age to the point where people studying them are lost in their ability to judge the age of the elders. Even at this age, the people are acute of mind and self-sufficient. It has been determined that the single most responsible factor is the diet, which is totally natural and fresh. They are, perhaps luckily, unaware of monosodium glutamate!

As to the importance of diet, consider the new born baby which can live and grow and be healthy surviving totally on its mother's milk. Nature has developed this source of nutrition to be singly able to provide a healthy life for a child. We all know, of course, that we have the ability to make formulas which certainly keep a child alive nutritionally. Nature, and nature alone, through mother's milk is able to pass on to the child certain immune capabilities.

My point to all this is that man has become very learned concerning nutrition but God and nature are forces to be reckoned with. Science does not know all the answers.

Why then, with the known and accepted fact that nutrition plays an all important role in the health and well being of the human body, do the powers that be in the United States scoff at the *possibility* that a natural herbal product *may* play an all important role in at least one serious health problem afflicting a high percentage of citizens?

Is it so difficult to believe that if a calcium or protein deficiency can be alleviated by adjustments to the diet using common foods that the *possibility* exists to alleviate the symptoms of arthritis with foods that may not be common to us? The Chinese, among other cultures, do not have "hang-ups" on the use of herbs in their daily diets. The use of herbs has been practiced for some 5,000 years. The use of herbs is as common to them for certain purposes as our drinking milk for its calcium benefits.

This, however, presents a problem.

Are herbs food or are they drugs? It is a much more difficult question than it seems on the surface. If herbs (or milk, for that matter) were advertised and sold for a therapeutic purpose they are then a drug as interpreted by our FDA. I personally like Hipocrates logic, "Let your food be your medicine, let your medicine be your food."

Arthritis is one of the oldest diseases known to mankind. Skeletal remains of prehistoric man have been shown to have suffered the effects of the disease. Over 40,000,000 people in the United States today suffer from this horribly crippling and extremely painful affliction.

Billions of dollars have been spent on medical technology studying the disease. Countless drugs, therapy's, devises, and synthetic joints have been invented and used in an attempt to alleviate the symptoms and the pain. None have been the answer!

The cause and cure is as elusive today as it was when the caveman's most effective weapon was a club. Modern science is wonderful: polio has been made a thing of the past, and penicillin saves many lives. Why now, working with neutrons and atoms, we have gotten so smart that we have the capability to destroy the earth as we know it.

The arthritic, however, still lives in as dark a cave as his ancestors concerning his disease. Sooner or later, after all drugs and therapys have failed, the arthritic is told by the medical community, "you must learn to live with it."

This book is the story of Richard J. Anderson, an arthritic for twenty years who refused to give up and "live with it."

Suppose for a minute that a product were available that has beneficial effects, reduces or eliminates pain, reduces or eliminates joint swelling, increases mobility and has *no* known dangerous side effects. Suppose further that this were the effect found by almost 100% of the arthritics who have used the product.

If this were to be true and known to our government agency the FDA, would it not be at least morally wrong to refuse arthritics the right *to decide for themselves* if they wished to try the product?

Well, there is such a product! A Chinese family's secret recipe of processing 22 various herbs individually and in combination was made available to the public in Hong Kong in 1974. The translation of the Chinese name for the product is "Chase the wind from the bones."

A person would think if all the above were true the good news would make the headlines all across the country considering the millions of people who could potentially benefit.

The exact opposite has occurred! The benefits have been totally suppressed. Worse, it has been called a potential killer containing various "dangerous" prescription drugs and toxins. Millions of taxpayers dollars have been spent to keep the product out of the U.S. and to prevent the public from learning about it.

Let us examine the prescription drug accusation. A news release by the FDA in December 1980 stated that this product contained the dangerous drugs listed below making it an illegal product. The list published was composed of the drugs dexamethasone, cortisone acetate, indomethacin, chlordiazepoxide and hydrocortisone plus the toxins lead and cadmium.

Pretty scary! Especially to a layman whose first impression is to accept as *fact* anything written and published by the FDA.

Surely this powerful agency could not be wrong! Yet, the statements below made by highly respected prominent people prove that "mistakes" are sometimes made:

Grover Cleveland in 1905 said "Sensible and responsible women do not want to vote."

Charles H. Duell, Director of U.S. Patent Office in 1899 said, "Everything that can be invented has been invented."

Robert Millikan, Nobel prize in physics said in 1923, "There is no likelihood man can ever tap the power of the atom."

Lord Kelvin, President of the Royal Society, c. 1895 said, "Heavier than air flying machines are impossible."

Well, mistakes can be made! In this case, should we believe 25 or so laboratories *all* made mistakes when they reported "no drugs" or is it easier to believe the FDA has made the mistake?

Now, on with Mr. Anderson's story.

J. E. Breslin

Chapter 1

Thank God we live in America. This, my fifth day in jail, has given me time to reflect upon my life to this point. Although I am in jail, I do not believe I am a criminal. The officers of the law who put me in this position know I am not a criminal. I have, however, refused to "roll over and go away" as they would like for me to do. I am here because my lawyer made a mistake and convinced me to do something totally against my better judgment. Perhaps in the long run being called a criminal has a way of working out for the best.

The founders of the United States of America were themselves criminals in the eyes of the strongest power in the world, England. These founders met secretly which was also known as a criminal conspiracy to plot against English rule. These criminals became the heros of the world, because what they were doing was for the good of humanity. No force on this earth could stop them because they were right.

One of my customers once wrote me these encouraging words, "Wrong must fail, right prevail." These words along with my dedication give me the courage to fight against all odds. I *will* win or die trying.

What exactly is arthritis? Chances are if you are reading this book you *know* what it is. Pain, pain and more pain. I would be interested in talking to any arthritic who at one time or another did not consider suicide as a way to stop the pain.

If you have not experienced this pain, I will attempt to describe it. Have you ever had a toothache? The kind where it literally drives you insane? Show me the person, no matter how frightened they may be of the dentist who doesn't immediately overcome this fear and beg for an appointment. How lucky you are! About 99.9% of the time the pain can be relieved almost in minutes.

Now use your imagination. Consider the size of your tooth, maybe 1/20th the size of your knee, 1/50th the size of your hip? Multiply in your mind the toothache pain you have experienced by 20 or 50 times and move it from your mouth to your knee or hip or any other joint in your body, maybe in *every joint*.

This time you go to the doctor. He says, "There is very little I can do, go home, take 3 aspirin every 4 hours. If you are not better in a week come back and see me." Oh, you'll be back, in worse pain plus upset stomach and ringing ears. Now starts the vicious circle!

Chapter 2

"Dick, if you keep that up you will get arthritis like Aunt Alice!" "Aw Mom, I'm strong, see I can carry kids bigger than I am. It doesn't hurt." Just try to tell a kid of about 10 years what to do or not to do. I certainly paid no heed to Mom's advice.

Like most of our family, I'm a small fella. Full grown, I had to stand very straight to hit 5'5", and that may be stretching a point. But that's all right, perhaps good things come in small packages. At the very least, I have never bumped my head going through a doorway!

As a kid, I did have one problem: broken fingers. For a couple of years, I wore a cast on one hand or the other almost constantly. Finally Doc Bradford said, "This boy has a calcium deficiency make him drink more milk." Well, I like milk anyway, and I now drank two glasses with every meal, two glasses in between meals and two glasses just before I went to bed. For at least a year this regiment was followed, along with a huge appetite. I grew no taller but have not had a broken bone since. That milk must be wonderful stuff!

Many a night, however, I was stiff of joint and sore of muscle. As active as I was, never stopping work or play, it was thought anyone could expect to be stiff and sore.

God bless Mom and Dad; five children kept them busy for many years. Two of my sisters and my only brother suffered with rheumatic fever, each spending months in hospitals. It seemed forever there was a hospital bed in the living room during recuperation at home. Never a day when one of her children was in the hospital did my mother fail to be there, even though we lived 10 miles from town. How she took care of the home and provided love and understanding for the four kids at home, I'll never know.

My father worked for the railroad plus farmed his 120 acres in an effort that we might live as well as possible. With all the normal expenses of raising a family plus the hospital and doctor bills, I don't know how he did it.

Part of what I have just said is not totally true, I *do* know how my parents did it. They had a faith in God and belief in Christ and the Church that was unshakable. From this faith, they went through life with a smile on their face and a song in their hearts. They taught us children what they believed to be true. They could not force me to accept all they taught at face value, but they did enforce learning. If nothing else, we learned by absorption, as they lived their lives as examples. I may have rebelled, but I learned and have never forgotten what they taught us.

Chapter 3

Like most kids, when I graduated from high school, I left home to seek my fame and fortune. I drove myself 320 miles to Minneapolis. I had $32.00 in my pocket and was rarr'in to go. I thought to myself, "Boy, this is not fair, every place I go for a job they ask about my experience. What? I just got out of high school, true, I worked at filling stations washing cars for two years. I had worked for farmers driving tractors and such. This wasn't the experience they had in mind. I was getting desperate. I walked down University Avenue and starting in St. Paul, I applied for work at every single place for miles. By the third day, I was worn out and worse, I was running out of businesses. Then the last place before getting to the University, I heard the words, "You can start in the morning."

They started me at eighty cents an hour; I was in clover. During the year and one half I worked there, I was promoted to manager and earned $1.25 per hour. I turned nineteen, and I got married the next day. Three months later I was trying to figure out why I couldn't get ahead. I thought that life should be so fun and so easy! My father used to tell me of the boy who at age sixteen couldn't believe how dumb his parents were, and who at nineteen could not understand how they got so smart in three short years. Well now I know *that* boy real well. Perhaps I should have listened a little closer.

Chapter 4

I eventually enlisted in the Navy. This way I could get an education and get paid at the same time. Two days after I left for boot camp, my wife was taken to the hospital; she was diabetic but the disease had been under control since we were married. As it turned out, she spent almost every day for six months in the hospital. The Red Cross and the Chaplain advised that I apply for a hardship dependency discharge as the Navy did not wish to pay the ever mounting medical bills. I was given an Honorable discharge after about six months of military service.

I did not think much of it at the time, but all through boot camp with the rigorous training, I hurt all the time. In the beginning, all the fellows were stiff and sore but got over it quickly. I did not, but thought it was possibly my small size and putting forth great effort to keep up.

Once out of the service, I convinced a furniture store I could handle their truck driving delivery service. I spent eight hours a day working physically hard, and another four hours at night being taught the selling end of the business. I was kidded about being the best dressed truck driver in Minneapolis. I wore dress clothes and necktie everyday to be mentally ready to meet customers in the evening. Being dressed this way was great for my self-image; I saw myself as a salesman, and was determined to be the best. We did not deliver on Saturdays so I was able to spend eight hours "on the floor." Months went by, and I was very pleased with my progress in becoming a salesman. Although I did not receive a dime for my selling efforts, I learned a great deal.

I began having trouble getting out of bed in the mornings. I was so stiff and sore I had to "limber up" before I could move properly. And why not, I thought, I'm working about seventy hours a week! Finally it got so bad that I decided to go to a doctor.

Following many tests and several appointments, he informed me I had arthritis. He gave me a prescription, and

I had it filled but found no relief. I became worse and worse. Finally I could not carry my weight performing my duties as a driver and delivery person. I went to the owner, who knew I was having a physical problem, and asked if I could become a full time sales person. He said first he would have to find a driver to replace me, would I train one? Sure I would! The only problem was he never did hire one.

My right heel was constantly causing pain, 24 hours a day. I began walking with a limp to compensate. I began looking for a job as a furniture salesman. This, I decided, is what I want to do with my life. The sales personnel made easily twice the money I did as a truck driver, yet I knew I was selling roughly the same dollar amounts they were. I felt ready to give it a try. I applied at many retail stores. In all but one case, I was told I did not have sufficient experience. The department manager at a large department store at Southdale, the largest shopping mall in the world at that time, agreed to give me a chance.

I gave it my all. I'll brag just a little;

I was one of the top three salespeople every month. My right heel was causing a big problem: it now stayed swollen all the time. I bought shoes one size too big so I could get the right one on. Then I had to cut out the back of the right shoe. My limping to compensate began causing me backaches. Weekly chiropractic adjustments helped. The doctor kept telling me I must have something done with my heel or I would ruin my back.

I also was seeing a M.D. during this time. He gave me prescriptions for pain. I tried to take the pain killers only in the evening when I came home from work. They made me groggy and lethargic, but I was able to sleep. One day while waiting for a prescription to be filled, I braced myself on a cane rack to get the weight off my right heel. I'll never forget choking back tears as I bought that first cane. I was twenty-one years old!

The M.D. finally told me he was unable to help me and gave me the name of a podiatrist. She examined my foot and had me fitted with a pair of corrective shoes. That shoe caused more pain, I believe, than the problem itself. God how it hurt. It caused me to put my weight on the arch rather than the heel. After three days I went back to see her hoping something could be done. I was told to take the pain killers and continue wearing the shoe as I could expect some discomfort in the beginning. About a month later with no relief in sight she said she could not help me and referred me to an orthopedic surgeon.

Following examination and x-rays the orthopedic surgeon said surgery was the only way to alleviate the problem.

I have gotten ahead of myself. Just prior to the surgeon I resigned from my sales position. I physically could not stand and get around the sales floor. I had been studying the insurance laws and received my license. I set up office in my home to avoid walking more than necessary. Financially it was tough going for a while building a business. But never one to expect things to come easy, I worked hard. My teacher gave me a formula to make a living in this business, "Make a hundred phone calls, expect to make ten appointments then you can expect to make one sale. Decide how much money you want to make and make phone calls accordingly." It worked, and of course with practice, one becomes more efficient. I made a decent living, we bought a house, owned two cars, and had a baby girl we named Susan. Other than my physical problems, I had it made.

Orthopedic surgery was in its infant stages at that time. Following surgery, I was in acute pain for quite a while. I asked the surgeon what I could do for the pain in the rest of my joints. By this time I ached all over. Knees would swell, elbows would swell, hands would swell, and my neck and back were constantly painful. "You will some day be a complete cripple," he told me. "There is no cure for arthritis!"

He suggested I move to Arizona as some arthritics do better in the dry climate.

Chapter 5

I sold the house, furniture, and both cars. I bought an eight year old De Soto from a friend to make the trip.

I paid off every bill so I could start with a clean slate. As I drove away from Minneapolis, I had $175.00 in my pocket, a wife and a fourteen month old child, and the clothes on our backs. No prospects, but a chance at better health.

I was still on crutches part time. By the time we reached Phoenix five days later, I was so stiff and sore from the long drive that I could hardly move. We checked into a tiny motel on Van Buren Street. It had a pool out front and a cheap price posted. It looked like heaven to me. The first thing I did was get in the pool. It was August 31, 1963, hot and I do mean hot!

As I sat in the pool relaxing my aching joints, a feeling came over me that I was home.

The next morning, I awoke feeling better than I had in three years. Not a pain in my body! I thought, "Look out world I'm ready to go."

It was not easy. Jobs were just not available. Employment agencies sent me here and there and all around the valley. After four days I hit the streets.

I figured I found my first job by applying at every business, and that I could do it again. Besides that, I was out of money and could not buy gas for the car. I started walking and applying at about 32nd street. Every motel, every restaurant, every service station, if it was a business, I applied. It took a few days, but my foot was better and I felt good, although I was worried about minor things like feeding my family and myself.

At Central and Van Buren, I got lucky. The manager at the Standard Oil station said I could start training the following Monday. The training location was at 17th avenue and Van Buren about four miles from the motel. I walked there in the morning and home at night. My only fear was that I would be assigned to work at a far away location following training. I knew that the first paycheck would not stretch. Fortunately, they put me at the Central and Van Buren station. I worked hard to do the best I could do. It paid off, and after about six months, I was promoted to lead salesman, and then to assistant manager at the largest station in the valley at 44th and Camelback.

By this time I had bought a home in northwest Phoenix. Life was pretty darn good for this little country boy!

All during this period, I was physically active in various sports. One of my real pleasures was to take my now two year old daughter out to the desert. There I would walk with her for miles. I learned to love this desert where I had regained my health.

It was too good to be true! One day I noticed a slight pain under the arch of my left foot. I didn't think much of it at first, but with each passing week, it got worse. I went to a M.D. to have it checked out. X-ray showed nothing but believe me it was very painful by the time I decided to see a doctor. He told me it must be in my head as he could find nothing wrong. He accused me of being a slacker, wanting to get time off work. Needless to say, I did not go back to him. What was worse, I put it off and began limping again to compensate.

Problem or no problem I must have been doing something right. An executive from Standard Oil took me to lunch one day and offered me an opportunity to own my own station. I was thrilled to death. I needed only (?) $1,500.00 down payment. At that time it seemed impossible, but I said, "Yes, I can arrange the down payment."

Chapter 6

A prouder twenty-four year old has never been than I was that October morning in 1964 when I unlocked the door to my first business. I was in debt to my eyeballs but that was ok, because nothing could stop me now.

I worked hard, opened at six a.m. and closed at nine p.m. seven days a week. My left foot pained, and I limped, but I couldn't worry about that right then.

After about two months, I was forced to start worrying about my health. The joints all over my body became stiffer and stiffer, and I ached 'til I thought I could not take it anymore. Finally, one morning, I could not go any longer without relief. I opened the business but literally could not get out of my chair to wait on customers. A sixteen-year-old boy rode in on his bicycle and offered to help. I hired him on the spot, showed him how to ring in cash, and left the business to him as I drove down the street to a D.O.'s office.

My whole body was so out of shape

from pain and the effects of limping that the doc just shook his head. The first thing he did was put me on a roller table. You lay flat on your back and a roller from under the table rolls up and down your spine. I laid there and cried from pain as it began to roll.

"You must take at least one week off from work," the doctor told me. Well there was no way I could do that so he gave me a prescription for pain pills and told me to take three aspirin every four hours. I did just as he prescribed but continued working. It was that or lose my business!

Mondays and Thursdays I was adjusted by that roller table. I learned to love it. Although it hurt like hell the first few minutes, I would begin to relax and actually fall asleep as it drove away some of my pain.

Now what? One morning I awoke and coughed up blood. My tummy had not been feeling good for some time, and of course the doctor told me aspirin would do this. I was told I must stop the aspirin. Prescriptions for anti-inflammatories began. Every one of them cause some sort of discomfort ranging from headaches to blood in the stool. It is an understatement to say I felt miserable.

Unfortunately, I had another problem all these years. I'll be brief. My wife had spent more than three of our seven year marriage in the hospital. Her diabetes was constantly uncontrolled.

A son had been born, proudly named after myself, nicknamed Rich, and of course I had my beautiful daughter. Due to the extended hospital stays of my wife, it was necessary for me to arrange baby sitters, do grocery shopping, and clothes washing. I'm afraid I finally gave up. I filed for divorce.

A short while after the divorce, a lady drove into my business. She had a problem with her car and was referred to me. I fell in love at first sight. Within the year, we were married, and I became step-father to her four children. I loved them as my own. They ranged in age from one and a half to twelve. God I was happy, in love with my new wife, and now I had six lovely children.

There was one minor problem. I was paying child support and alimony to one ex-wife and now had five more people to feed and clothe. Looking back, I must have been brave.

I knew the answer. Make more money! I bought out the service station across the street. I had customers going to work in the morning at one station and caught others going home at night at the other.

The strain of all this on my body was showing. I had bought out a customer's carpet cleaning business along with his house. We moved into the almost new home, and I rented out the small two bedroom place I had bought when we got married. Three businesses and the one rental proved too much. The D.O. did his best to keep me walking, but by now the left foot had developed a lump under the arch. I guess the M.D. who said it was all in my head was mistaken.

The two younger children would take turns massaging my foot and my back each evening. To them, it was a game of playing doctor, but I can tell you true, the love that passed through those massages helped me keep going.

I kept a cane at the service stations,

but I was careful not to let my new wife and kids see me walking with it. I did not want them to know that I felt like an old, old man most of the time.

A small incident at my second station gave me a new project. One young employee shorted out a customers alternator while installing it. When it shorted a lot more than twelve volts happened. The breaker bar actually was welded to the exhaust manifold. The new alternator was ruined, so I laid it on the shelf, installed another new one, and forgot about it. I swear I woke up in the middle of the night and thought, "How could it be?"

I sold my first station and went to work trying to figure out what caused the high voltage welding on that alternator incident. It took many hours of diligent work to figure out not only what happened but how to make use of the power.

Once I knew how to do it, I designed a small unit which attached to the alternator. A switch allowed anyone to run power tools and many other appliances from under the hood of their car. A special made cable set allowed light welding and fast battery charging. Sales were great. If only I had no pain!

I found an orthopedic surgeon who performed surgery on my left foot. How stupid I was to let it go so long. Following surgery and recuperation, I naturally did not have to walk with a limp. Soon I was a new man.

I opened a carpet sales store to run in conjuction with the carpet cleaning. I learned how to install carpet wall to wall. I was not satisfied until I was a master at it. Then I trained two men to do it so we would have satisfied customers every single time.

My Auto-Volt manufacturing of the alternator gadget was going well. I hired physically handicapped people to do the assembly work. I had applied for a patent and was excited about the potential.

I decided to sell the remaining service station when my right heel began giving me problems once again. The pain was just to much to even think about trying to stay up with everything.

I bought a bar thinking it could be run with hired help. That turned out to be one of my genuine mistakes. I certainly was not mentally equipped to handle the problems that go with that type of business, or at least the one I owned.

In 1971, I was thirty-one years old and back to walking with a cane, in pain every day. I went back to the orthopedic surgeon, and he scheduled surgery for the right heel, this time the left side. While laying in the hospital, I felt tired of the whole thing and made a decision. I would give my carpet operation to my friend who had worked hard to make it a success. I would sell the bar and the Auto-Volt business. The bar was a break even situation only, and I wanted out and literally gave it away. The patent office declined my application, because it was not a novel idea, although they ruled it was a novel application. Novel ideas only are patentable. I really believed I would make it big with the Auto-Volt and was crushed when unable to patent it. I had a buyer lined up for one million in cash plus royalties if I could provide the patent. Oh well, the best laid plans of mice and men oft' go astray.

I had made some money and learned alot. I sold out for the cost of materials plus a small blue sky and walked away. The patent attorneys wound up doing much better than I did financially.

With about one years living tucked away, recuperating from surgery, I went to real estate school and also took pilot's training.

School was to become able to make my living in a less strenuous manner, and flying was for pleasure.

Sometime prior to this, I had bought and fixed up an old boat. All the children were taught to swim, run the boat, and water-ski. With some time off from work we "lived" at Lake Pleasant. I felt great most of the time. Without the stress of business ownership and the long hard hours of physical work, I had no pain at all, sometimes for a week or two. Small flare-ups really don't count; they are liveable.

Chapter 7

We skip now to 1979. Several changes have taken place in my personal and business life. My arthritic problem has been more annoying than serious for about eight years. Flare-ups sometimes would last 2 weeks, sometimes 2 months, but the disease would go back into remission.

I had gone through another divorce and re- married again. This time to a lovely young lady. She really managed quite well considering my oldest step-daughter was older than she. Having a total of 6 children (although mostly grown and gone) was not perhaps the easiest life for her, but I loved my children, and life was good.

During the first week in September 1979, I awoke one morning remission gone. God, I don't guess I ever hurt that bad. I could not get out of bed by myself. Every movement caused so much pain, I thought I would die. I was used to flare-ups in one knee or the other, one hip or the other but never like this. Starting at the base of my neck, I hurt in every joint in my body.

My wife filled the tub with hot water then helped me from the bed to the tub. I very slowly worked the joints until they loosened up at least a little bit. Over the years I had developed a high tolerance to pain, but how I made it to work that day I'll never know.

I was, at the time, sales manager of the light duty truck department of General GMC in Phoenix. This company had seen me come to work many times during the eight months I had been employed, walking slow because of a knee, ankle, hip or spine, being stiff and sore. They, like myself, thought a week or two would find me back to normal.

By the third day, I had to go to the doctor. I had no luck at all with aspirin. I took so many my stomach burned, my ears rang and my head was fuzzy. Anti-inflammatories were started. Indomethacin, clinoril, and a host of others were prescribed. Hot packs and cold packs were tried. Pain killing shots were given. Cortisone and procaine were injected into my left heel where the most acute pain was centered, although every joint in my body was painful. At night my knees would lock, *any* slight movement was an experience in pain.

Four doctors, a D.O., a Podiatrist, a Chiropractor, and an Acupuncturist tried to help me to no avail. After the second adjustment, the Chiropractor, seeing tears rolling down my cheeks as he tried to work stiffness out of my spine, stopped and said, "Dick, I can't help you." I hobbled back to my vehicle on my cane. I painfully got myself situated behind the wheel, and then, for the second time in the span of minutes, I cried again, this time in despair.

The D.O. had tried all he knew and had referred me to the Podiatrist for the acute left heel pain. Ultra sound, and shots and prescriptions for anti-inflammatories continued. Finally butazoladin alka was prescribed. The relief found with this drug was slight but the best so far. I had two days of pills and when they were gone, I went back for more. The doctor refused, saying they were dangerous unless very carefully prescribed. This drug has recently been removed from the market due to the many deaths it has caused. I tried to tell him that I didn't care if I died tomorrow, if I could just have a minute's reprieve today. He said to come back the following week, and he would give me more.

The Acupuncturist had me lay face down as he placed about 60 needles from my neck to my toes. After close to an hour, he removed them. It may have been in my mind, but I thought I felt a little better. Later that night, my left heel began to burn. It felt as though an actual flame was under it. I bore the pain all night, and by morning it had subsided slightly. I called him and explained. He told me it was probably a good sign, and that if he could drive the pain from the rest of my body to that one area, we were on the right track. After several treatments, I knew it was not the answer.

Well meaning friends brought me home remedies from all over the country. I ate alfalfa sprouts and tablets, I drank raw goat's milk, I took megadoses of vitamins E & C, panothenic acid, calcium supplements, pau d'arco from Brazil, chinchona, honey, pollen and propolis tablets. I tried raw honey, and God knows I tried anything and everything!

A Mexican lady brought marijuana. She boiled it into a strong tea, soaked terry towels with it, and wrapped my knees and ankles. She talked softly and hummed to me and kept the hot towels on me until the wee hours of the morning hoping I could relax and get some much needed sleep. God bless her she tried, but my pain would not subside. The next evening she brought more marijuana, but this time she made me a cigarette thinking that might relax me. Unfortunately, that made my stomach queasy and slowed down my senses. The slightest movement was exaggerated in time making the pain seem to go on forever. Believe me, marijuana is *not* the answer.

I, to this day, have no experience or desire to experiment with illicit drugs, but during that time, I would have given them all a try.

Another friend heard of DMSO. Many arthritics have sought relief with this product by applying it to painful joints.

He could not find any in Phoenix so he flew to Wisconsin and smuggled a pint back to me. It was considered illegal at that time. Other than a horrible taste in my mouth seconds after it was applied, nothing happened. I hurt just as bad during and after the treatment as before.

I am *not* a slacker. I went to work every day. I could not make it up the four steps to my office. Ten salesmen worked for me so there were always two of them available to carry me. Some days I could not get from my home to my vehicle, and a phone call would bring two of them to get me.

I had a hot water spa installed in my back yard. Every morning and every evening found me sitting in 104 degree water. The heat and bouyancy helped just slightly while in the water. Once out, the benefits were gone.

On December 31, 1979 I turned in my resignation as sales manager. I could not physically or mentally go on. Surprisingly, during the four solid months I was so sick, we set sales records, and I believe some of them still stand today. My men saw the effort I put in just to be on the job; they in turn put forth their greatest effort. As a team, we clicked.

Now I sat at home every day spending hours in the hot spa. I'm afraid I became sullen and very depressed. I'm thirty-nine and one-half years old chronolocogically but ninety plus in physical ability. I realized I was not the best thing that could happen to a lovely, twenty- four year old wife. Although we loved each other, my mind was not attuned to love or the responsibility that goes with it. She worked for the telephone company putting in her hours and then would have to come home and tend to my needs. I *hated* being dependent upon her and made it a point to alienate myself from her.

It was not easy, but I succeeded in driving her away. She kept coming home; I kept sending her away. There are people who to this day can't understand how she could leave me in that condition, or why I will always love her, but believe me, that lady did not give up easily.

Once I got her to leave, I started taking a loaded gun to bed with me. Every night I vowed to myself that *that* night when I awoke in pain from the slightest movement, I would end it all. As you know by reading this book, I did not bring myself to actually committing suicide. I do not know why I didn't. It certainly was not a fear of death. I found myself envying friends that had died of cancer. True, they had suffered terribly, but they had died, relieving their pain. Sitting at the beside of one such friend, I asked him to fight for life as I did not want to lose his friendship. He said if I were his friend to pray for his death. I did; he died that night.

No, death is not the enemy. We must, to fulfill Gods plan, fight for life, but when the time comes for death let us welcome it as merely an extention of life of a better kind. Remember, "cowards suffer a thousand deaths, the brave will die but once."

Arthritics don't die of the disease. We pray for remission, we pray that medical science will tomorrow discover a cure, we pray tomorrow we will feel better. "Maybe tomorrow," we pray.

The management at General GMC had a meeting to discuss how they might help me. I was approached by one of the managers. He made a good argument. "Hurt at home or hurt at work, at least you will make a living." Most large companies would welcome being rid of a person in my condition. Not this company. They gave me a sales job in the motor home division with a desk on the ground floor. They had not accepted my resignation, but turned it into a leave of absence so I still had insurance. Yes, I love these people, and hope I have proven myself worthy of their friendship and concern.

February, March, and April, I made a good living although I had not had one minute without pain in eight solid months. My spirits were better while interacting with customers and friends. My wife insisted I let her come home. If only I could have just one day without pain!

Chapter 8

Miracles? Sure, we have all heard of them. They happened in Biblical times, and we all know the stories. In fact, the word miracle finds its way into many a conversation.

I do not know if *you* believe in miracles but please read on.

On May 5, 1980, I went to work as usual. At about 1:15 PM one of my friends came back from lunch. He came directly to me and said, "My wife's sister is in town, visiting from L.A., I just had lunch with her and noticed her taking some little pills, I asked what kind of vitamins they were. She said "Oh, they are not vitamins, they're Chinese herbs I take for my arthritis."

In his hand he had a small package, "I bought a package from her for you to try, if you will," he told me.

Does a drowning man reach for a straw? For eight months I reached for every straw that floated by, although discouraged by all I would have laid in cow dung if someone said it might help!

The instructions he told me were to take six pills that evening. I did about 6 PM. I went to bed, exhausted as usual, about 10 PM.

Chapter 9

It was the most vivid dream. I could see the sun shining through the bedroom window, the drape was lazily swaying in the breeze, birds were singing in the tree just outside, and the temperature was perfect. "This must be heaven. Where am I?" I thought.

I dared not move. I felt totally comfortable. I moved my eyes, I was awake. No, that was not possible; something was very different. I slowly moved my arm to reach for my cane. The movement did not hurt. I very slowly moved my left leg towards the edge of the bed, no pain. I followed with my right leg, still no pain. I am dreaming, no, this is real life. I put my feet on the floor, and I reached for the door knob to pull myself up. Not necessary, my body followed my arm. I was standing. I bent over to reach my cane, no pain. I looked back at the bed. I fully expected to see my physical body still there. "This must be death, if so it is beautiful," I thought. I took a step, then two, another, no pain. I walked in a daze, although my mind had never witnessed such clarity. I was fully aware of every nerve in my body, waiting for each to scream, "you're hurting me!"

Once in the bathroom I looked in the mirror, and there I was, a smile on my face. A cry escaped my lips. My wife jumped out of bed and ran to me thinking I needed help. "Look," I said, "no pain."

I sat down on the edge of the bathtub and cried. I buried my face in my hands. Emotion like I have never experienced before or since flooded over me. My wife hugged me and cried with me. We wiped away our tears, and I stood up and walked to the kitchen, then the living room, getting more excited with each pain free step.

Although I am not a religous person like my father and mother, I have a deep faith in God, the Almighty, or by what other name for a superior force is in the mind of man. I sat on the sofa and prayed out loud to my God. I thanked him from the bottom of my heart for answering my prayer.

I hurried through my shower and shave. I couldn't wait 'til 8 AM to get to work to tell my friend what happened.

I walked into his office, straight, shoulders back, no cane, a smile on my face. "Jim," I said, "look here," I did perhaps the shortest lasting little jig ever, "no pain."

His mouth was agape. I walked to him with tears in my eyes, hand extended and said, simply, "thanks."

We laughed, and we cried. Jim said, "Dick, do you realize this is the best birthday of my life!" As coincidence would have it, it was his birthday. It may have been his best birthday, but let me tell you, I had lived exactly 39 years, 11 months and 1 day to reach this point, and it was the *BEST DAY OF MY LIFE.*

I feel I could go on and on trying to describe my feelings, but I don't want to bore you with details. If you are arthritic, you can visualize my emotion.

About 3 PM that afternoon, I began to ache. God what fear overtook me. Jim called home and talked to his sister-in-law. Take six in the morning and six in the evening I was instructed. I took six pills right then, and by 5 PM I was having *no* pain again.

Then the biggest fear of my life took place. I only have forty-eight pills left. That's only four days. Jim called his sister again, and she sold me another package and gave me the phone number in Los Angeles. I called, but it was too late, and they were not open. At 8 AM the following morning, I was on the phone. No answer. In a panic, I called Jim. "L.A. is an hour behind us in time," he told me, "Wait until 9 AM."

I guarantee my fear now was not of death but of living without these herbal pills. I could hear the phone ringing, and finally a heavily accented Chinese ladies voice answered. "Buy the pills, yes, of course, how many?" I was asked. One hundred packages I told her. "Not possible," she said, "send a cashier's check, you can have six packages."

The bank was my next stop. I mailed the check. For about six days, I was nervous. A package came in the mail, six packages of life itself were in my hand. I sent another check. More pills came; I sent another check, more pills.

I sent double the money, and double the pills came back.

I calculated if I lived to be eighty years old how many pills I would need to stock up and the cost. The figure was about $30,000.00. I did not have that kind of money, but figured I would buy all I could as quickly as I could.

I told everybody I saw of my good fortune. My friends told their families and friends of my good fortune. Soon people were calling the store for me, others came to the store, dozens of them. Something had to change. The store was overrun with people to see me: the miracle case. I supplied any arthritic who wanted to try with a package with the address of the L.A. supplier. The first to try was Marvin Buttenob of Sun City. The morning after he got the first package my phone rang at six in the morning, getting me out of bed. "Dick," the crying voice said, "this is Marvin, I just combed my hair with my right hand for the first time in years, thank you, thank you." God what a feeling, but I did nothing except make them available to him.

The typing of this manuscript is taking place almost exactly six years since Marvin called me that morning. I want you to read the letter I received from him about one week ago. It is a precise reprint; I have the letter in file.

Randisco, Inc.
3011 W. Palo Verde
Phoenix, Az. 85017

Attn: R.J. Anderson

I am 71 years of age. It is extremely difficult for me to understand that the FDA has put a hold on your EARTH'S MAGIC inventory.

Permit me to relate my experience relative to using various medications as prescribed by my doctor. I was diagnosed as having rheumatoid arthritis and my doctor put me on motrin. I still had pain to the point where my wife had to help me put on an underwear top plus the shirt. Meanwhile after three years usage blood began emitting from my backside.

My doctor took me off motrin and put me on nalfon. After approximately 1½ years I began losing blood via my mouth. I was sent to an ear, nose and throat specialist whose diagnoses was ambiguous. In any event I discontinued taking nalfon. The medication was not eliminating pain any more than motrin had.

My doctor then put me on feldene. After a period of taking feldene for approximately 6 months my doctor, through blood tests primarily checking for liver performance informed me that my liver performance was somewhat alarming and stated I should cut my usage by 50%. I immediately discontinued using feldene.

I have ever since been using your product herbs and EARTH'S MAGIC. My golf handicap dropped in a relatively short period of time from 17 to 12. What a difference being pain free makes.

Also my doctor (same one through the years) several weeks ago ran a blood check. He told me my sed rate was virtually normal, kidneys and liver are excellent, also blood pressure 136 over 80. He also checked the lungs and heart with no problem there.

I cannot understand what goes on in America, here I had nothing but severe side effects while taking various prescription drugs. Meanwhile your product has eliminated pain with no side effects. Even my doctor is amazed at the transformation of my health to the positive side.

Sincerely and honestly,
Marvin Buttenob

Nearly 2,000 similar letters have been received from all over the country. I receive more almost daily. Most of them would make you cry!

Chapter 10

Dozens of people had begun buying the herbal product from the Chinese people in L.A. through my referral and that of others.

One day in August of 1980, a man called me. He sounded frightened to death. "Dick," he said, "the supplier in Los Angeles has gone out of business." I told him, "No, that can't be, I just received an order."

Thinking perhaps they had just taken a vacation or maybe were sick, I was not upset. I called Jim, the friend whose sister-in-law introduced me to the herbs. Jim called her and asked if they could find out what was going on.

The news stabbed me with uncontrollable fear. The store was closed with no forwarding address.

I was in a panic. I dug through every scrap of paper that had come with the packages. They had been wrapped in newspaper, and fortunately I had saved every scrap in a box. Why, I do not know. The newspaper scraps were in Chinese. An advertisement showed the picture of a little dark ball, and by God if it didn't look like the pills I was taking. I could just make out the Hong Kong phone number.

I was scheduled to work, but called in and said I could not make it in that day. I believe it was a first.

With the help of an overseas operator, I began calling. By now it was about 9 AM. No answer. I dialed, as I recall, about sixteen times that day. No answer! When my wife (a telephone operator) came home that afternoon, I was a nervous wreck. She said, "No problem, let me help." She called work and immediately found out that there is a sixteen hour time difference. I had been calling in the middle of the night in Hong Kong. She figured out what time here would be 8 AM there. I called then, and the phone was answered by a Chinese voice, speaking Chinese. She could not understand English. I was about to go crazy! I called again 9 AM their time. Again, a Chinese voice. I tried to explain, and the phone went quiet for a moment. "Hello." The voice was in English! "Yes, we manufacture the pills."

Sweeter words have never been uttered. "Send cashiers check, we will send merchandise."

When the bank opened for business the next day I was the first in!

Chapter 11

As the word spread concerning the supplier, people came to me asking what to do. I had, as I mentioned earlier, been stocking up. I had perhaps a two or three year supply for myself by this time. The others had not done this.

"Please," they begged, "can we buy from you, we will pay any price." I said, "I cannot do this for money, I only want to help." I sold from my stock at my cost in the beginning with no thought of turning it into a business. It seemed morally wrong to make a profit from the disease I had suffered with for so many years.

Many of these people got together and approached me with this theory. Collectively they had, over the years, spent hundreds of thousands, perhaps millions of dollars with doctors looking for relief. These doctors were not doing it for free. They had found relief with this herbal product. If I made a business of it, they would buy from me and happily pay me a profit, so I could expand it and make it available to more and more people.

This made good sense so I went to work. First of all, I decided to have the product analysed. Although it did not make common sense, skeptics thought it must be dangerous to be so effective. Perhaps, they said, it is full of drugs!

I, and my new found fellow arthritics had been prescribed every known drug with little if any relief. All of a sudden we were all finding ourselves pain free. I had now taken twelve a day for four months. I had regained lost weight, regained my strength, had *no* pain, was full of ambition, and good health literally glowed from me and the other users.

For myself, I did not care if it were made with rat poison. However, selling it to others, required some prudence. I thought the emminent authority would be a major University.

This is the report following analysis from ASU Department of Chemistry:

Dear Mr. Anderson:

This constitutes my report on your arthritis medication. I have performed an infrared spectroscopic investigation of your medication, with the particular goal of identifying cortisone. All these tests for cortisone were negative. It is my conclusion that the contents of this medication did not contain cortisone and that the components therein *are natural to the herbs* detailed in your ingredient list.

Respectfully submitted,
M.L. Parsons
Consulting Chemist

Prior to this I had been acting on faith, but I now proceeded with confidence. Merchandise was coming from Hong Kong. On September 20, 1980, I made my first retail sale. Thank God for my prior business experience. I obtained the necessary business licenses. I was legitimately in a new business. My prices were a small mark-up, just enough to pay expenses. Although I could visualize tremendous potential, I could not bring myself to actually making money from others pain or even relief from pain. Some aquaintances thought me terribly naive!

Strange! All my life I had chased the almighty dollar; I wanted to become rich. All of a sudden I had found greater wealth than I knew existed. Freedom from pain and the gratitude of *many* people who were also free of pain. My billions of dollars worth of wealth can be found, not in the bank, but in the more than 1,000 letters I have in file from customers thanking me for making this herb available to them.

When it comes my time to die I hope my epitath can read:

Here lies
R.J. Anderson
The richest man in the world.
He did his best
and gained the respect
of his fellow man.

God, I could cry. That's beautiful, if I do say so myself!

Seriously, it's a good thing money was not my motive. Had it been I would have quit a long time ago considering the problems I have encountered.

Chapter 12

Did I mention the good word spread quickly? At the end of September, I closed the books with about $550.00 total sales. October more than $3,000.00, November more than $5,000.00.

December hummed along. On the 16th, I got up as usual about 6 AM, got the newspaper and headed for the spa with my cup of coffee. I learned to love that spa when I needed it just to survive. Now it was merely used for sincere pleasure.

An article catches my eye. "FDA finds drugs in Chinese herbal product touted for arthritis," the headline read.

I would have liked to have died on the spot! I read on. "Linked to the death of an elderly woman. Contains dangerous drugs and toxins, lead, cadmium, dexamethazone, cortisone acetate, indomethacin, chlordiazepoxide, hydrochlorothiazide and hydrocortisone."

It was too early in the morning to do anything, but I jumped out of the spa and headed for the bathroom to get ready. I did not make it. The phone rang, and it was Marvin. "Yes, I have read the story." I started again for the bathroom. The phone rang, another customer then another and another. By this time, my wife was awake from all the ringing of the phone. She began answering it, while I showered telling everyone to call back later.

While showering my mind was racing, what to do? When I finished dressing, I got on the phone and called the FDA office in Atlanta where the story stemmed from. It was later there so they were open although it was only 7 AM in Phoenix.

"Does linked mean caused?" I asked, I was told, "No, she had taken the pills, she did die, so they were linked!" "If she had eaten peas prior to dying would they also be linked," I asked. "Yes," was the answer. I was beginning to understand.

A few weeks before that, I was called to the home of a man who told me he suffered terribly from arthritis. Although I had never gone to anyone to sell my product, (people came to me), I made an exception when told he could not get around. Upon arriving, I was let in and brought to the living room. The very tiny woman, who looked worn out asked me to sit while she got her husband. She went through the arcadia door to the back yard and called him. Walking toward me was one of the most obese men I have ever seen. Once in, he sat down in his chair and proceeded to tell me of his great pain. To tell the truth, his little wife looked much more harried than he. "Get me this, get me that." At least six times during the half hour I was there, he *ordered* his wife to get something for him. When he spoke, she jumped. He bought a month's supply. I am not used to anyone being treated as he did his wife and was glad to leave. He called when running low and told me how wonderful he was feeling and wanted me to bring more. I told him to put his check in the mail, and I would send the order.

A local television station, doing their civic duty picked up on the FDA news release story and included it in the 6 o'clock news the evening of December 16. The man described above called the channel and said he was taking the pills, and that he almost died! Cheryl Parker of the station went to his home and interviewed him the next day. She then came to my home. I was at work and didn't know that any of this was going on and left at the end of my shift. Upon arriving at my home, I saw several people talking on the street just beyond. I saw them walking towards me, and then Cheryl Parker asked if I was Mr. Anderson. I said yes, so she identified herself and the cameraman. She expressed surprise when I invited them into my home. "I am more than happy to tell my story concerning the herbal pills," I told her naively.

I showed her the ASU lab report, and I showed her the doctors report following my comprehensive physical proving my physical condition to be perfect. She then told me she had just interviewed "obese man." Cheryl Parker said he told her he had almost died! I took his record out of file and showed it to her. "Does it seem reasonable that a sane human being would order a second time if he almost died from them?" She had no answer for the question. As she left, I felt good that at least my side would be told.

I could have cried if I were not so angry as I watched the news that evening. She told a story alright! "This poor, poor man almost died, he bought pills from Mr. Anderson who did not tell him they were full of drugs and dangerous. If you are buying pills from this man stop taking them at once or *you* may be his next victim."

I called another local station the next morning asking if they wanted to interview the biggest seller of Chinese herb pills in the state. You bet they did. I asked only that they be fair in telling the story. Todd Benjamin and a cameraman came to my home that afternoon. The news report on that channel at least softened the blow from the night before. The best part was the Dave Nichols commentary, something to this effect, "if those pills are a killer considering Mr. Anderson has taken thousands of them he is the healthiest dead man I have ever seen."

Chapter 13

It is a good thing that I stayed working for General GMC selling motorhomes. Income-wise my little herbal sales business went in the toilet! Well, that is not exactly true. It did, however, drop way down for a while. And why not, if people are told they are going to die from some pill, it's pretty scary. Especially if the FDA says it plus a big powerful corporation like the TV station!

New business was what slowed down. Customers from young to old called me to offer encouragement. People are not as gullible as sometimes thought. We see TV news, we read newspapers we hear what we are suppose to hear. But we commoners are not totally dumb! We have that important quality known as common sense. My father used to say, "believe none of what you hear and half of what you see, then you will be pretty close to the truth."

I could see trouble a comin' so I decided I better put on my thinking cap and beat'm to the punch. If I had a laboratory analyze samples from every shipment proving no drugs, I would be immune from legal problems, right? And so I did. Only one *big* problem. I called lab after lab. "You're Mr. Anderson, the man with the killer pills," they would ask? "Stay away from our lab, we don't want trouble with the FDA! ASU Chemistry Laboratory said they were happy to analyze any product but were not in a position to do it on a commercial basis.

Finally I reached Vern Bolin, the owner of Bolin Laboratories, Inc., "bring me samples," said this gruff, matter of fact voice, "bring them, don't send them."

"When?" I asked. "Right now" he said. Betcha your life I brought them, right then! I got off the phone and headed to his lab.

Quite a guy, this Vern, about my size and just as tough as nails. (like me) "What's the problem?" he asked. Well, I bent his ear for about half an hour telling him about FDA claims of drugs, and showed him ASU report and medical report of my condition. "I'm not scared of those (beep-beep)," said he. "Leave your pills and list of drugs and toxins with me."

The report came in as follows:

Lead	none detected
Cadium	none detected
Dexamethasone	none detected
Cortisone Acetate	none detected
Indomethacin	none detected
Chlordiazepozide	none detected
Hydrochlorothiazide	none detected
Hydrocortisone	none detected

"Gotcha, FDA," I thought. "I know just what to do, I'll type a nice letter explaining *my* Chinese herbs. (which I had named APRH TEA BALLS, the letters representing Arthritis pain relieving herbs, a mistake, as you will see later.)

I wrote to the effect that *my* product could not possibly be the same as the one in the newspaper article! "Please see the attached scientific lab analysis proving *no drugs.*" I sent a copy to the FDA and the Maricopa County Health Department. I figured that I was pretty smart and that I would head them off at the pass.

Wrong! Another article hit the papers. "Herb pills from Hong Kong linked to death of San Fransisco man in *1974*" (this is *1981*). New drugs are added to the list.

Off I went to Bolin lab with a new list. Guess what? The report came back *ALL NEGATIVE.*

I went to an attorney, and (first of many, you'll see) gave him all the information. He checked out what I told him and showed him. "Looks ok to me," he said "but I better check further." He called the FDA and they informed him, "What Mr. Anderson is doing is not illegal but we advise him to cease operation." He called the head man at Maricopa Health Department. They said, "What Mr. Anderson is doing is not illegal but we advise him to cease operation."

You get the feeling these birds were talking together? About me?

Well, I ain't too big and I ain't too smart. My Mom taught me, "son if you are *right* don't back down!" Hey Mom, did I learn good? My little experience at boxing taught me if you get in the ring, you damn well better be prepared to *fight*. Hey coach, did I learn good?

My attorneys have told me "Let sleeping dogs lie!" That's not dumb advise either, but like I told you, I ain't all that smart!

Many labs checked for drugs in APRH TEA BALLS during the next year. Guess what? *Every* one of them was negative. I felt pretty smug. I guess I showed them!

Dr. Meyer of Parker, Arizona became acquainted with the herbs in a strange sort of way. One of his patients, a lady in her eighties bounced into his office one day. "Look doc," she said, as she did a mini-jig, "I guess I don't need you any more."

Well doc's a tough ol' bird also. He is as big as I am small, well over 6 feet! Tough or not when he saw this old lady the last time she was crying in pain from her arthritis, just like she had for years. He had treated her to the best of his ability, using the 50 years of experience plus the most modern drugs and therapies at his disposal.

Seeing her like this made his mouth

drop open as he slowly sat down in the chair. "What the heck is going on?" he asked her, having *never* seen anything like it in all his years of practice. "Well, my sister came to visit from Phoenix because I have been is such pain, she wanted to help me. Just before she left town she heard someone talking about the relief they got for their arthritis with APRH TEA BALLS. So she bought some and brought them to me. It's a miracle, my pain is gone!"

Doctor Meyer got on the phone and called me in Phoenix. I got a little scared. Why is a doctor calling me? "I want to meet you," he said. "Well come on," I answered.

Two days later, he was at my door. An hour's conversation later, he talked me into letting him buy the product from me and distribute it to his patients.

I was thrilled that a doctor had taken interest in the herbal product. Many other customers when telling their doctors about the relief they found with APRH TEA BALLS were told it was dangerous, and they should stop. A few people did stop because they were scared. The huge majority, however, rationalized that if the pain were gone and *no* side effects were apparent, it could not be very dangerous. Especially when they knew the drugs prescribed by the doctors *did* have side effects and certainly had at least the potential for danger.

Now I had a medical practitioner who could do clinical follow-ups on people taking the product. A three and one-half year study proved the safety and efficacy of the product. In almost 100% of the cases the pain went away and stayed away while taking the APRH TEA BALLS. In some cases, people were able to discontinue usage after a time and remain pain free.

Shortly after Doctor Meyer became involved, a serious legal problem arose.

Chapter 14

Approximately the first week of March of 1982, a lady from Awatukee (suburb of Phoenix) whom I will call "Ellen" heard from some of her neighbors the wonderful results they had obtained by using APRH TEA BALLS. Having suffered greatly with arthritis for many years, she called me and ordered some.

I have never met this lady face to face, but I was told by her and her friends the transformation was wonderful to behold.

In the beginning, her daily phone calls stating her desire to become a distributor were merely annoying. Hundreds of people have made the same request. With this one exception, all those wanting distributorships understand when I tell them the controversial nature of the product prohibits me, in good faith, from doing this.

I explained to her that even I had not taken my first dollar from the company for personal use. I worked full time in a sales position to make my living.

Finally after three months, her request had turned into a demand. I *must* let her distribute to make money, she insisted. One evening, about May 23, 1982, I told her she must stop calling daily. I *would* not make her a distributor, and further more, if she did not cease calling for that purpose, I would no longer fill her orders. I pride myself on my patience, but her roughly sixtieth call had strained it to breaking.

The next evening she was taken by ambulance to a nearby hospital. She claimed that she was deathly sick. The hospital, however, could find nothing wrong. At her insistance, they transferred her to another hospital. There she said she was probably overdosed on librium from the APRH TEA BALLS. (Clordiazepoxide is the generic name for librium.)

Dave Jallum, the spokesman for the hospital came on the 6 o'clock TV news the next evening holding a package of my product saying, "These pills are full of librium, if you're taking them stop and see a doctor immediately, they are dangerous!"

Again, this was pretty scary information. I have hundreds of customers in the area, and I believe every one of them called me. Almost everyone said, *"I DON'T BELIEVE THEM!"* These people were, of course, knowledgeable of the fact that my analysis *proved* different.

Several of "Ellen's" neighbors called to tell me their view of the situation. This lady was *not* their friend. She is an overbearing person. One lady, a professor, said she probably *was* overdosed on librium, but if so had taken that drug on her own, because she was out to get me for not letting her sell my product.

Cheryl Parker, the news reporter (the same one who interviewed me) went to the hospital with a cameraman to get the story. On the evening news, it went like this, "I am Cheryl Parker, do you remember when I interviewed this man, (my picture is shown) he is the one who sells APRH TEA BALLS, I warned you before what might happen and now it has, this poor lady almost died last night, overdosed on librium from Mr. Anderson's pills. They are killers, stop taking them." (Then the interview) "Ellen would you tell in your own words what happened?" "Yes, I took APRH TEA BALLS for three months, I knew something must be wrong as I felt better than I had in years. Then last night I just collapsed." Cheryl Parker: "Are you angry with Mr. Anderson?" "Yes," said Ellen, "he is making all that money off people."

I have in my possession her complete file while hospitalized, which I obtained when I, out of necessity, became my own attorney many months later. The problem she experienced, according to several doctors who checked her out, was malar flush (red cheeks), lethargic, and painful joints. This file is about seventy-five pages long, and there is *no* mention of *any* drug substance being found in blood or urine analysis. She later admitted in a deposition to my attorneys that she was not sick, and that she just hurt from pain and that she had stopped the APRH TEA BALLS when I said I might not sell them to her anymore.

At a later date, this hospital's laboratory, at my attorney's insistance, analyzed my APRH TEA BALLS. Guess what? *NO LIBRIUM!* I have copies of their results proving this.

I wish the adverse publicity was the worst of the problem, but it was not.

An investigator from the Arizona Department of Public Safety (the DPS) was called to interview the lady in the hospital. Criminal drug selling charges were filed by her against me. The DPS obtained samples from her.

About two days later, I got a phone call from an "arthritic". He wanted to meet me, and asked if he could come to the house? "Yes, of course." I told him.

You know the feeling you get when something does not ring true? Well, I have spoken at length with perhaps 1,000 people suffering from arthritis during the previous two years. I "feel" their pain and anguish, even over the phone. This voice did not ring true.

For two years, I had been living with a certain fear that some form of official pressure would be brought to bear.

Upon arriving at my home with his "nephew", who I was told was skeptical due to all the bad publicity, a briefcase was carefully placed on my desk.

They wanted me to try to "sell" them the APRH TEA BALLS. I can truthfully say I have never tried to "sell" anyone the product. I make it available to anyone who wishes to purchase it of their own free will, period.

As an inducement to "sell" them, they referred several times as to being skeptical. Finally I stood up from behind my desk and made the statement, "I have no interest in selling you a product which makes you scared." I made as though I were going to show them out. At this, the young man said "Oh we're not that scared. We will buy some."

I had the older man fill out the order form with his name and address. He did not want to do it. I said, "Fine, let me just put away the package of herbs." "You mean you won't sell them to me?" the man asked. "Not without your name and address," I told him "my business is mail order because I work out of my home, plus I keep exact records on everyone of my customers." He reluctantly filled out the form.

I "knew" there was a recorder in that briefcase, so I made a point of going over the ASU and Bolin Laboratory reports proving that the APRH TEA BALLS contained no drugs. I also gave them copies of the lab reports.

When they left, I looked at the order form, checked the phone book for a match, and called the number. A lady identified herself as the housekeeper. She gave me Jim Treadgill's (the older man) work number. I dialed the number, and it was answered, "Narcotics division, may I help you?" "Yes," I said "when Jim Treadgill comes in please have him call R.J. Anderson, I want him to know that in the future they can come like men not mice. I will be happy to supply the State with samples of my product. They do not have to use taxpayer's money to buy them."

Beyond this point in my story, you will feel a degree of cynicism concerning my feeling of law, order, and justice as actually practiced by officers of the law.

Please believe, however, that I love and respect the United States of America. Where, I ask you, could a person such as myself put up such a fight, as I have, against the State and Federal Government? In many countries, I would be merely shot or thrown in jail to rot!

There have been times when incidents took place where I felt this *might* happen.

Chapter 15

The months of June, July, and August in 1982 were much slower business-wise. This is for two reasons, I'm sure. One is that arthritics seem to suffer less in the summer months, and the other is that the end of May found my picture and that of my product frequently on TV news with false but scary stories.

On about the 20th of August, I received a strange phone call. A "redneck" sounding voice said, "Hey man, you the guy that sells the black rabbit shit that you say are good for arthritis?" "No," I said "I do sell APRH TEA BALLS." "Well I've got some information for you," I was told. "You have some heavy trouble coming down." "Do you work for the DPS?" I asked. "Never mind who I work for, I've got information you will want." I didn't like this conversation at all. There seemed to be a veiled threat behind every word. To put an end to it, I said, "OK what's the information?" "Man, you are dumb, this information is worth a bundle, we can arrange a meeting place, you have cash, you get the info." I'm afraid I lost my cool and told him what he could wipe with his "info".

I may be wrong but I would, yet today, bet a dollar to a donut that this man was from the DPS.

I must, prior to proceeding with the story, relate some events in my personal life during the very trying time with adverse publicity. I became a man obsessed with the need to continue making available the herbal product regardless of the pressures involved. This obsession led to inattention towards my wife. I must admit I failed to realize that her needs and desires needed fulfillment also. This, plus the strain of living daily with the threat that some sort of legal problem was emminent, resulted in divorce.

Good things often stem from what at the time seems unbearable.

As good fortune would have it, in April of 1981 I met Judie. She had supported and raised two children to young adulthood by herself for many years. Her children were nineteen and twenty-three at the time we met, and I am *most* happy to say that no man ever had a stronger bond with his children than has developed between us.

Judie knows from first hand experience the value of dedication and hard work to get a job done.

Had I been granted a "wish upon a star" I could not have done as well. She is one in a million!

Chapter 16

Another strange phone call came on August 23, 1982. I was getting used to these calls that did not ring true. One morning at about 6 AM, the caller identified himself as Mike Taylor, saying he suffered horribly with arthritis. He asked if he could buy my pills. I said, "Please give me your phone number, I'll call you right back, someone is at my door." By now I know the prefix number of the DPS. Sure enough, I called later in the day, and asked for Jim Welty who had been· to my home "undercover" and later I discovered was a DPS detective. "He is out right now, can I take a message?" No, the message was loud and clear; they were trying to "trip me up."

You see, if I make claims for the product, it is then classified as a drug, and I am not licensed to sell drugs. Therefore, I do not advertise my product or tout it in any way. If people want to try it, they must take the word of a referral or decide themselves. I cannot legally "sell" them on trying it, and I do not.

Anyway, many strange calls came through almost daily. This one man said, "I suffer so bad, I'm from Michigan, I'm at a friends house in Mesa, the lady here is having such good results with your product. Can I come over and buy some?"

When asked the lady's name he could not think of it at the moment. Ah, ha, I had him pegged. I knew he was "undercover". That was alright, because every time they came over, I gave them an increasing number of analysis of the product proving that it contains *no drugs*. Perhaps I was too confident, but why not, I had about eight analysis from about four different laboratories, and *all* the results of the tests stated *no drugs*. I would like to point out that some of the labs used are nationally located and used by the medical profession to analyze patient's blood, urine and biopsies. I figured if they are good enough for doctors, they are good enough for me. After all, they have the health of Americans in their hands.

Ten or so minutes after I got off the

phone Mr. Stocksdale drives up. (Mesa is 30 miles away?) Poor fellow, he limped so badly walking up to the house. He bought the product, was given lab results, and headed back to his car. This was a real miracle: his limp had gone away! As he got in his car I said, "God bless you."

My gut feeling that something was about to break was not long in proving accurate.

Two days after Mr. Stocksdale's visit, my daughter, Staci called me at work. "Dad, you better come home right away!" The sound of her voice needed no explanation. I jumped in my car and drove straight home.

Wow, the "gestapo" was out in full force. As I pulled onto my street, both ends were blocked off by cars, effectively containing me. I guess they expected me to "run". Well not on your life! I pulled up in front, parked on the street, and got out of the car with a smile on my face. I still was full of confidence. I did have proof my product was legal.

A total of about fourteen men converged on me. Why, can you believe it, some were my "arthritic friends." I cockily walked up to three of them, offered a handshake, and complimented them on their apparent good health. I'm afraid they could not see the humor.

They escorted me into my home telling me they had a search warrant. "What charge?" I asked. "Possession and sale of the dangerous drug Librium." I was told. "You are quite mistaken, you have many analysis obtained from myself which disprove that." "Your analysis are no good." said Jim Welty, the "nephew" who was the first undercover man to come to my home three months ago.

"But Bolin Lab for one is a highly respected local scientific lab."

"Bolin Lab is no good."

"Let me ask you a question, do you drink Phoenix City water?"

"Yes, but what does that have to do with it?"

"Bolin Lab is certified and used by Phoenix to analyze city water for impurities. If they are good enough for the City, how can they not be good enough for me?"

"They are no good."

"How about ASU lab?"

"They are no good."

"How about National Health Lab?"

"They are no good."

My confidence began slipping.

"We are going to search your home and confiscate anything we deem appropriate under the search warrant, you can help or we *will* tear your house apart. It's up to you to co-operate or not, we don't care," Jim Welty stated. "At this moment you carry the big stick so I will co- operate," I told them.

Hopefully you have never had your home violated as mine was that day. All fourteen or so men begin searching. Although I said I would co-operate, I could not be in all rooms at all times. I personally took them to every bit of stock I owned, more than $10,000.00 in value. Hundreds of dollars of undeposited checks, every single paper in my entire office, even personal records such as house payment cards, tax records going back years, etc. were taken. I begged them to leave at least the items necessary to fulfill my obligation of paying bills. "Evidence" I was told. They took everything!

Now this was all bad enough. I figured they were in control, so I stayed calm.

That was until I heard Jim Welty and Dave Rubin in the dining room, a deputy county attorney, questioning my daughter at the table. Jim Welty was asking her if she slept with me! Now it just so happens, this 20 year old girl is beautiful by any standard. All the time, these "law officers" were there, leering looks and comments were commonplace. I could live with that. Hearing this question, however, blew my patience, and I stormed into the room and strongly, verbally objected. A heavy hand took me by the shoulder and having my daughter leave the table *forced* me to sit and be subjected to the same line of questioning.

This is not the "law, order, and justice" I was taught to respect and did for forty years. As I write this, I feel something important was stolen from me that day, not the dollar value, dollars are replaceable. If I drilled anything into *all* my eight children's heads, it is that respect is *earned* and not available or obtainable by any other means. Well, that day representatives from our government agencies, the DPS, Post Office, and FDA and perhaps others, plus TV reporters and cameramen were in attendance. They all seemed to think my outrage was humorous.

Upon getting ready to leave after about three hours, I was expecting to be taken to jail. I steadied my nerves to accept it. "Oh, we're not going to arrest you, we are going to give you the benefit of the doubt," stated DPS detective Jim Welty.

Once again I was outraged, "You mean you have "sufficient" evidence to come into my home, 'steal' my property, but do *not* have enough evidence to arrest me and charge me with supposedly selling dangerous drugs?"

Believe me, I was relieved at not being arrested, but I realized then it was their desire to 'scare' me out of business as they were certainly lacking in evidence. I have yet to hear of another case where a man was accused of selling dangerous (State's terminology, includes librium) drugs and not arrested on the spot.

That evening and for the next several days, TV news (same station that 'blasted me' previously) bragged of how the DPS made this big "drug" bust on Mr. Anderson, "You remember him, the one with the killer pills." Many times in a restaurant or other public place, people could be heard whispering, "There's the man who was busted for drugs." This went on for quite some time. I *had* exposure!

Funny thing, I was degraded and thought a criminal by many, *except* my customers. They called with encouragement, they sent letters of encouragement, and some called DPS telling them of the unfairness of it all. They *should not have to suffer.* I was, by the way, back in business the day following the seizure. I wasn't all dumb; I had expected a problem for a long time. I had merchandise stored in various places. I merely went to one of my warehouses and picked up more merchandise. Orders come by mail, and every order received was filled at once. Business took a big jump! For the first time, adverse publicity *brought* customers.

I did feel it necessary to now resign from General GMC. As good as they were to me, I could not bring any possible degration to their doorstep. (They *are* good people. I recommend you buy your next pick-up or motorhome from them. Some employees are my *best* friends!)

Chapter 17

A firm of attorneys were hired, not to defend me, as there had been no charge. I hired them to fight back, and prove my product is legal, so I could have the seized items returned to me.

At our first meeting, I showed them the multitude of analysis that had been performed proving no drugs, including librium. (Remember this is the same as chlordiazepoxide). They recommended I stay in business, give them a $10,000.00 retainer, and let them go to work. And so I did.

One of the things I did finally opened my eyes. I called the FDA office in San Fransisco. This office was responsible for stopping many of my shipments of the herbs as they came through customs. I recorded the conversation so I could go back over it later.

The FDA compliance officer and I talked for about forty-five minutes. Finally, when it seemed I would never understand, he told me, "The problem is *not* what the product may or may not contain, the problem is that it is being bought and sold as a therapeutic aid for arthritis. *That* makes it a *drug* in the eyes of the FDA."

"I have sold this product to more than 1,000 people, no side effects, I have had it analyzed by many laboratories, no drugs. You mean to tell me that although it contains no drugs, it is a *drug* due to the fact arthritics buy it and find relief?"

"Now you're getting the picture, if it is going to be used and sold for this purpose you must first obtain a NDA (new drug application). If it is approved *then* the product will be legal."

He then cut off the conversation as he had a terrible toothache and had an appointment with the dentist. I could not refrain from telling him how lucky he was. *Any* dentist can relieve the pain of a toothache likely to *never* return. Arthritics are not so lucky. *No* doctor has the ability to stop the pain. Even if it is slightly relieved, it *will* be back and back and back. *WE ALL KNOW THERE IS NO CURE FOR ARTHRITIS.*

He sent me a copy of a NDA. It takes

five to ten years, and $10,000,000.00 to $20,000,000.00. That's bad enough, but the catch is that a drug can have no more than three compounds. The herbal product has twenty-two herbs plus honey. Our laws are such that this product *cannot* be made legal in the United States. So suffer arthritics. Although help *is* available for a high percentage of you, the FDA says it is illegal!

My tenacity may result in jail but I will not believe it will keep me out of heaven!

What I am doing by making this herbal product available may be contrary to law as perceived by officers and agencies of our government.

I feel I must answer to a higher authority.

I have sold this product to thousands of people who bought it of their own free will, and I have received thousands of letters of testimony as to the benefits obtained. I do *not* get complaints!

Compressed, this is my goal: Citizens of the United States should have the right *to decide for themselves, of their own free will, if they would try this product or at least be made aware of it.*

If the medical profession, or the FDA, or the drug companies have a better alternative let them now speak or forever hold their peace!

I have customers who range in age from their teens to 90's. I am aware of three deaths of customers during the past six years. One man committed suicide during a shortage of the product caused by the DPS seizure, another, while working his farm, was killed in a tractor accident, and another died of a heart attack. Several family members of the heart attack victim called to thank me for providing a product which allowed him his last months on this earth to be pain free!

Is this herbal combination a killer? I have tried and tried and hoped and hoped to have a jury trial. I have paid attorney's nearly $200,000.00 to take advantage of this *right* under our constitution. But to no avail. I have been prosecuted and persecuted for almost six years as this is typed. Both the FDA and the DPS have, by "legal manipulation", prevented a trial from taking place.

I only ask, let twelve of my peers decide the issue. Since this has not been allowed, I ask you, the readers of this book, (hopefully more than twelve) *you* be my jury. I *will* abide by your decision. You the citizen *are* the law; *you* are the government. Is this not how our great country remains the best in the world? *WE ARE A FREE NATION*, or are we?

Please read the following letter. This lady has been a customer for several years:

To Whom It May Concern:

Letter writing is not a talent of mine, it is something very hard for me-I don't even write to family and friends if I can help it. However, I do feel compelled to write to SOMEONE on behalf of Mr. R.J. Anderson and "Earth's Magic".

I don't know who I should be truly grateful to, GOD or Mr. Anderson-I'm sure both, for giving me four years of "Living" again after many years of "Hell". I am 48 years old and have Rheumatoid Arthritis-not one or two joints in my body are affected but my total body. I have been the usual route beginning with M.D.'s right on up the ladder, and the usual beginning of aspirin right on up-taking one anti-inflammatory 'til side effects appear and then another and another. A "vicious" circle as all arthritics know. Doctors all giving up and saying there's nothing more to be done. Gold injections were last resort.

I had to hire a lady to clean for me as I could no longer perform household duties. I couldn't begin to get down on my hands and knees-if I did manage it, I couldn't get back up. I remember wanting to plant some flowers so bad but couldn't kneel down so I managed to get myself in a sitting position and literally "scooted" around on the ground to plant the flowers and then when I was finished I couldn't get up. I sat there for what seemed forever as no one was home and finally rolled myself over on my stomach and managed to somehow get myself up off the ground. This was only one of many experiences of being totally helpless over my own body.

One day, the lady I hired to clean

for me, knowing of the pain I was having, mentioned about the new "Herb" medicine that her Uncle started taking and what a "Miracle" it was for him and that he was doing things that he hadn't done for years, gardening-etc. Only people that have been there realize that you will do and try ANYTHING that might possibility alleviate constant pain. As Mr. Anderson mentions in his book, a toothache you can contend with, even maybe one or two joints but when your whole body is wracked with pain, you certainly do not look forward to a new day beginning, you just want relief in any way, shape or form-harmful to your body or not-you don't care-just please God relieve this pain! I don't care how!

I asked my cleaning lady to get me the name of where her Uncle got these "Herbs". Naturally, my family thought what a bunch of "quackery" and probably, truthfully, so did I but I was grasping at anything!

I received the samples I sent for and my God, I was born again! With one dosage, MY MIRACLE happened. I could barely walk down my stairs in the morning and by the evening after taking six tablets late in the morning, I felt like I could go jogging with my son! Do I care what's in these pills????? Would you? If I lived six months, one year or whatever, I didn't care what I was taking because I finally was receiving some relief and I'll bet any arthritic would say the same thing if they were suffering like I was.

I have now taken these "herbs" for four years, 12 tablets per day. I have not suffered one side effect whatsoever-would you like me to elaborate about all the side effects I did suffer from PX medications I took prior-I think not! Would these side effects not eventually have killed me? I had blood work done about 6 months ago, testing for 35 different things-everything tested fine. Some might try to say that I am in remission which is not true because I know for sure if I happen to forget to take my "Herbs". I live in fear of the day when this might not be available to me and I'm sure I'm joined by many others living with the same fear.

I do not understand why the FDA is fighting Mr. Anderson rather than working with him to find out why these "herbs" are working so miraculously for so many people. Don't they want to help us? It is evident to me what the reason must be-many Pharmaceutical Companies would suffer wouldn't they??? As to the product Mr. Anderson is distributing-we are supposed to be a free world-We, the People, are supposed to have Freedom of Choice-and I, along with many others, choose to LIVE WITHOUT PAIN. Should I die tomorrow, I have at least had four years of my life revived for me thanks to Mr. Anderson and what he has fought so diligently for. This has been MY choice to take his product. I would go to the end of the Earth or whatever it took to support what Mr. Anderson has done for me, my family, and many other people and their families. This man does not deserve what he is being put through-he is only trying to help humanity. I wrote long ago to the Arthritis Foundation about this product when I first started taking it, THEY didn't even have the concern, or decency, to answer my letter.

Prove to me what is harmful in this "Herbal" medication. I, and many others have the right to know why we, the people, are going to possibly have this product removed from us and we have to go back to living a life of "HELL" once again.

If Mr. Anderson is to be taken to trial over this product, at least give him a a jury trial so We The People can be present and be living examples on his behalf!

Yours truly,

Dian

cc: Mr. R.J. Anderson
Frank Peake FDA
3718 No. 16th St.
Phoenix, Arizona 85016

Arthritis Foundation
National Office
3400 Peachtree Rd., N.E.
Atlanta, Ga. 30326

The White House
Washington, D.C. 20500
Attn: Nancy Reagan

I ask, who of you would have the intestinal fortitude to tell this lady "go to hell, I quit, it's too much trouble for me, go back to pain, suffering and walkers, I don't care!"

If anyone of you could do the above, stay away from me. I'll never be your friend, and I will fight you to the death. You can put this in the bank; I am a tough "son-of-a-bitch" (sorry to use this phrase, 'out of anger') and when we're done, you will know you have been in a fight!

I'll tell you what you *can* do. Pray your grandparents, or parents or you, or your children never get this disease.

God bless you, I hope your prayer will be answered because it is an accepted fact that almost everyone, if they live long enough, will at some point in their lives, suffer with arthritis!

Chapter 18

My attorneys collected samples from different lot numbers.

They sent the samples to various labs with the instructions, "determine the presence or absence of librium."

Within a few weeks, at least five reports were received, and guess what, they were *negative*. Well, how about that, even the hospital whose spokesman on TV stated my product was full of librium was forced to admit the truth (I have the report from them) that it *did not* contain the drug!

End of legal problem, right? Wrong. Although I was doing business every day, from my home, and receiving and sending through the U.S. Post Office, and had yet more proof of my products legality, I could feel in my bones that it wasn't over.

Strange and sometimes threatening phone calls were received. In the middle of the night, the phone would ring, and a voice would say, "I'm going to get you." Yes, I believe it was officers of the DPS. During the day, unfamiliar cars would be parked down the street, up the street, or across the street. If a customer came to my home, they were followed when they left. I was followed when driving away. Judie was followed, and my daughter Staci was also followed. Hard to believe? This man must be lying, you say. Not possible in the United States, you say? You will see.

Chapter 19

On January 2, 1983, I arrived in Los Angeles. I was driving my motorhome, which was loaded down with everything required to run my business. This was done so that I would have my shower, bedroom and kitchen with me. My home and my office were on wheels.

I went to California for two reasons. One, to be out of the jurisdiction of the Arizona DPS, as I knew by now they were out to get me "by hook or by crook". They no longer cared whether or not my product was legal. They had vowed to put me out of business and were determined to accomplish it. Two, I needed to spend time with Leung Lo. He is my herbal advisor, born and raised in China. He received his Doctorate of Herbal Pharmacology at the University of Bejing (formerly Peking).

I met this man I swear due to some superior force's (God's?) intervention. I met strictly by chance Joanne an eighteen year old girl from California. She drove a motorhome to Phoenix, delivering it to General GMC from the factory. This was in the fall, 1980.

I heard "Los Angeles" mentioned, and so I introduced myself.

How could I have known at that moment a lifelong friendship was about to begin.

While waiting for the necessary paperwork to be completed. Joanne and I sat facing each other over a coffee table in the showroom. Thoughts were racing through my mind, "This girl is from L.A. perhaps she can help me."

"How are you getting to the airport?" I asked. "I can take a taxi," was her answer. "Please, let me drive you, I have something I would like you to read." We left immediately.

Over coffee, at the airport, I handed her my first effort by way of letter to inform other arthritics of my story.

Here is what it said:

September 12, 1980

"My name is Dick Anderson, I am an arthritic. I know pain, I know it well. It was my entire life 24 hours a day from the first of September 1979 to May 5, 1980. I have had pain for the last 20 years but then it would come and go. I had three surgeries during the 1960's due to arthritis. When it hit me September 1979 I thought it would last a week or two but weeks dragged into months of waking up with excruciating pain trying to find a more comfortable position.

I was sales manager for a large dealer in Phoenix, Arizona when I got sick. After four months of trying to get around with every step painful I resigned. I could stand the pain NO LONGER.

I went to four different doctors, a Chiropractor, D.O., Acupuncturist and a Podiatrist. They each treated me to no avail.

The Chiropractor adjusted me after a full length x-ray. The pain was almost unbearable. He said it was to be expected so I made another appointment for several days later. As I climbed up on his table I had tears in my eyes from pain. He looked at me and said "Dick, I cannot help you." I left his office in despair not knowing what to do next.

The D.O. used hot packs, prescriptions and adjustments. It was suggested that I install a hot water spa at my home as heat did offer some temporary relief. I had one installed at a cost of $2500.00 and used it four to five times a day with water temperatures of 103 degrees. While in the water I felt somewhat better. The degree of weightlessness allowed me to do some simple exercising of my joints.

The Acupuncturist used needles in my shoulders, down the length of my back, lower back area, knees, left heel and right foot. A total of about 60 needles. Upon leaving his office I felt a little better, my shoulders seemed a little more relaxed, my knees seemed a little more mobile. I went home and relaxed for an hour or two when my left heel began to throb with a burning sensation. The pain was horrible so I called him and told him what was happening, he said the inflammation in my system was probably centralizing in the most susceptible area of my body. The explanation sounded reasonable so I bore the pain until the following day, then went and had a cortisone shot for relief. After several acupuncture treatments, with some degree of relief lasting perhaps twelve hours, I realized it was not the answer.

The Podiatrist gave me the shots of cortisone directly into my left heel. I had ultra-sound treatments in his office. I was given prescriptions for Butazolidin Alka, Endocin and many other drugs. He warned me of the danger of Butazolidin Alka as it is harmful to the blood making a person more susceptible to cancer. I begged him to give me more as I did not care if I died at some future date if I could have some relief today.

I believe the doctors were all acting in good faith but after spending thousands of dollars I was no better.

I also tried every home remedy that well meaning people offered. This included large doses of alfalfa, raw honey, organic juices, and many more. Needless to say nothing helped.

Then a miracle came my way. A friend of mine heard about a herb that relieved arthritic pain and asked if I were interested in trying them. I had been grabbing for straws for months and was willing to try anything. I purchased a bag of the herbs and took six after my evening meal. Upon retiring that night I slept the whole night through. I woke up the next morning, got out of bed without my wife's help, walked to the bathroom without my cane, and had no pain. My first reaction was total disbelief. I had not taken one step without pain for months and overnight felt like a new man.

I went to my friend and told him of the results-I should say showed him as I was able to walk, bend, sit, stand and do the things most people take for granted in just moving ones body without pain.

I must tell you that I have had days of pain since I began taking the herb. In the beginning I did not have enough to take the necessary amount morning and night. Therefore I hurt some until I was able to take them regularly.

In July, 1980, I met a doctor in the course of my work. When I told him my story he offered to examine me free of charge if I would go without the herbs for two days. I did and by the time I was at his office I was in terrible pain and needed help to get up on his table. The x-rays show that I have arthritis, so did the blood test performed the next day. Even though I took twelve herbs the afternoon and evening before the blood test there was not a trace of drug or foreign substance in my blood.

I have spent this summer vacationing in Mexico and San Diego, fishing, waterskiing, exercising, doing push-ups, sit-ups and putting my body back into its healthful condition. I have also worked as a recreational vehicle salesman where I walk on a large lot showing my product.

Today I am 40 years old and feel 20. One year ago I was 39 and felt 90 with nothing to live for.

I am a walking miracle as only another arthritic could possibly understand."

When she finished reading, she looked at me with a tear in her eye.

I proceeded to tell her the story, "Original supplier out of business, no forwarding address. I need someone to track the owners down, and/or, find someone in Chinatown, L.A. who would be willing to work with me.

Joanne said, "I'll do it!" The L.A. area is big, and her home was sixty miles from Chinatown. She went to Chinatown. She went to *every* store starting at one end. She asked, she cajoled, and she begged every storeowner to please talk with her. At the end of the day, she called me "no luck," but she was only half way through Chinatown. She said she would go back the next day and finish.

Tenacity, this girl owns a million shares of stock in that word!

Midway through the next day, she called me. "I found a place that has the pills." I was excitedly told. "How many bags?" I asked. "I don't know, I'll ask." I heard her talking to someone, obviously Chinese. "Seven bags." she says. "Buy them," I tell her "but question them how to find the people I originally bought from."

Well she questioned and questioned,

but they would not tell her, "Why?" she asked. "Big trouble, FDA closed them down, threatened them." they told her.

Now we know why they went out of business. We also knew at least some product is available in Chinatown, L.A.

She went to the next store and another and another. Finally at one store, an old lady said "no," they do not have it. She, the old lady, spoke to her husband in the back room. He came out and spoke with Joanne. He was very nervous and told her so. "How do we know you're not from the government trying to cause us trouble?" She called me collect from their phone. "Let me talk to them." I said. The old man got on the phone. Now I have told you that I am a salesman, but I have never "sold" anything as strong as I sold myself to this Chinese man. I convinced him I was not FDA. He agreed to talk with Joanne, and she came back on the phone. "Buy every bag they have," I told her "then call me back."

Joanne literally walked into their back room, and insisted on seeing how many bags they had. She counted them, forty -nine. "I will buy them all," she said. They would not take my signed blank check from Phoenix. Did she quit? Not this girl. She went to the nearest bank, cashed her own check for the amount needed (how many eighteen year old girls can do that?), returned to the store, paid cash, left and called me. When I heard that story, I loved her as my best friend.

She kept on going. At the *last* store in Chinatown, the *last one* selling herbal products and the like, she met Leung Lo!!!

Yes, he would be willing to work with me, but he would want to meet me first.

I do not know a single soul on this earth who would have done what Joanne did, and would you believe it, I had to *force* money on her in payment. She did not want money. It was a favor to a new found friend. I can only hope I am worthy of this kind of friend.

Chapter 20

Doing business from my motorhome in L.A. was easy enough. I merely called home each day and was given the names and addresses of orders received. With that, the orders were filled and sent the same day received as usual.

Although I had known Leung Lo for two years, this was the first time we had an opportunity to spend more than one rushed day at a time together. We began to see each other as friends, and have over the years, developed that into a best friend status.

Knowing that eventually my ability to continue importing the APRH TEA BALLS would surely cease from governmental pressure, I set out to "develop" the product myself.

"Nothing to it." I thought. I had the formula, freely given me by the Hong Kong manufacturer. Leung Lo had an inventory of each and every one of the twenty-two herbal ingredients ordered in for this purpose. He and I sat hour after hour grinding, mixing, and capsulating these ingredients. After two full weeks of working with the herbs and doing business from the motorhome, I left Los Angeles. I had with me an inventory of several thousand capsules of "homemade" APRH TEA BALLS packaged twenty to a small zip-lock bag, just like the original product.

My destination was Parker, Arizona. Dr. Meyer had now been working with the original product "APRH TEA BALLS" as I had named them for twenty months. He was convinced through clinical experience of the safety and efficiency of the product. The proof was in the wonderful, glorious relief of arthritic pain in his patients.

My idea was to present him with the homemade product. He could then run a test. Patients could be *given* samples of the "homemade" but would have to *buy* the original. If they liked the "homemade" just as well, they would be able to purchase it for about half the price of the APRH TEA BALLS.

Nothing in this world comes easy. Patients, it turned out, would rather pay twice the money and get APRH

TEA BALLS. Well, back to work!

After leaving Parker, I drove back to Phoenix. Living in a motorhome like a vagabond is wonderful for vacation, but for me the vacation was over.

Feeling in my bones that trouble was coming, I found a RV park to put my motorhome in. I used my little MG sports car to commute from my home to my "office on wheels."

I had been home for nine days, commuting to do business. Each day as I left the house, I drove around in a circuitous manner to be certain I was not followed. I would eventually get to the motorhome where I would fill orders, and then take them to the Post Office for mailing. It worked wonderfully!

Until January 25, 1983. That is a memorable date, as it was the 25th of August 1982 the first search and seizure took place.

I left my home as usual, and I literally forgot to look for anyone following me. I had breakfast at a restaurant, read the paper, and lanquished over several cups of coffee. Upon leaving, I drove straight to my motorhome.

I did not know it for a couple of hours

that I had indeed been followed!

I filled the orders, made up the bank deposit, made journal entries, and relaxed over a cup of coffee.

I took the orders, locked the motorhome, got into my car, and drove to the Post Office.

Chapter 21

How was I to know I was driving my last mile as a "free" citizen?

I arrived at the Post Office around 11 AM. I parked directly in front of the depository boxes. Sure, I noticed a car pull up on my right hand side to park. Nothing unusual about that. As I got out of the car, I sort of patted the beautiful sheepskin seat covers I had installed the day before. I love the old cars that I buy and fix up. The convertible top was brand new. I had installed new carpet, and the body was waxed to a high sheen. Yes, I was proud of it!

I walked around to the other side, opened the door, and lifted out the box filled with orders to be mailed. I 'bumped' the door shut, and had taken about three steps when the driver's door on the car that had parked next to me opened, and a voice said, "Are you R.J. Anderson?"

Rather surprised, I answered, "Yes, who are you?" as I did not recognize him. He showed me a DPS badge. I would be lying if I said I felt confident at that moment. My heart sank and at the same time doubled in beats.

"Are you aware you have in your possession the dangerous drug librium?"

"No, I am not aware of any such thing," I replied "to the contrary I have in my possession many scientific reports that *prove* no librium or *any* other drug, may I show you?"

"Set your box on the trunk of your car," I was told. I did. "Now put your hands on the top of your car, spread them out and spread your feet."

The 'oft seen posture on TV is just exactly how it is done, but believe me the feeling is different when experienced in real life. The officer was six foot plus, and he carried a badge and a gun. In my mind, I once again thought, "he has the 'big stick' and I will certainly keep my nerves under control."

"Consider yourself temporarily detained," he said as he searched me top to bottom. "Remain in that position while I make a call." He spoke on his car radio and I could hear voices answering him, all stating they were coming in.

Within a very few minutes, many cars converged in my immediate area. They were regular cars, nothing noticeable about them. From them emerged one or two men per car. If I say ten men total surrounded me, I would be very close to the truth.

"If we merely take the box of orders and let you go, will you cease this business?" asked Jim Welty, the DPS officer I am most familiar with. He was the 'nephew' who in May, eight months ago, was at my home. He was also the officer in charge August 25th at the search and seizure.

I am afraid that I felt a new surge of confidence, as I thought, "it does not sound as if they are going to, or even want to arrest me."

"Shame on you," I said "if you have sufficient evidence to 'steal' a man's property, but lack sufficient evidence to charge him with a crime, again, shame on you."

Well, so much for confidence. The 'detaining' officer was left 'detaining' me as the others huddled perhaps ten feet away.

My mind envisioned myself as a young football player weighing 130 pounds who was facing a pro team each weighing 220 pounds. When the huddle breaks with a game plan, they will slap hands in camaraderie, look at me with that menacing grimace, and charge. You bet I'm scared. My teammates are 'out to lunch'. Alone I awaited the crash of 2,200 pounds!

Chapter 22

Quoting William Buckley from an editorial that appeared in the Phoenix Republic newspaper: "the supreme humiliation is to be taken into a jail cell."

I must, speaking from my personal experience, differ with him.

I had lived in this neighborhood, at the time of arrest, for twenty years. For more than three years, I had been mailing products from this Post Office almost daily.

A crowd of curious people had gathered. As I was arrested and handcuffed, the crowd was told to disperse. "The excitement is all over." and officer tells them. "What did he do?" I hear one man ask. "This was a drug bust." the officer tells him. "Well, I'm glad to see you doing your job, I hope you get all those drug selling SOB's." the man in the crowd stated.

That, folks, was *my* "Supreme Humiliation." Contained in the packages I was about to mail was life itself for many, many people. One order was going to Dr. Meyer. Just that order would keep eight people pain free for one month. *That* was the sad part. I could live through the humiliation.

I was driven by Mike Taylor (one of my "in such pain" callers) to the DPS building. There I was put in a holding tank, small (3'x3') but clean. I forced my mind to reflect on a higher plane. Without this ability, I'm afraid I would have screamed, which no doubt would have pleased those whom I thought of as my tormentors. I certainly was not about to let them think I was broken.

I was 'booked' at this office. I did not have any notion as to what happened beyond this point. All I knew was that it seemed to take an inordinate amount of time to put down the pertinent information.

Approximately 4 PM there was a flurry of activity. I was put into a car with Mike Taylor. They attempted to put the seat belt on me with my hands cuffed behind my back. The belt would not fasten so the officer said "To hell with it," slammed the door, and off we went.

It was apparent that Mike Taylor was angry about something. He drove erractically, passing cars, speeding to beat the lights, and cussing other drivers. He missed beating one light and stopped so fast I flew forward. At this I said, "I'm already under arrest, must you *break* laws just to get me to jail?"

Chapter 23

Maricopa County jail, now there is an experience I could well do without. I agree, however, such places are necessary. Frankly, I felt much safer knowing the majority in this cell were locked up. I didn't want to meet them "anywhere" else. They were a tough, scary bunch. As the door clanked shut behind me, I felt fear for the second time that day.

First, when answering my question about driving recklessly Mike Taylor said, "You think you are so goddamn smart don't you, well we've got you now!" I replied, "No, this is just the first round, as long as I live I will keep fighting back because I *am* right!" "That's right, you're *still* alive aren't you?" I shut up because I did not like the connotation.

Walking into the cell, two unsavory appearing men looked at me closely.

One said, "Sure do like your shirt!" "Hey, nice shoes man," the other stated. Yep, they scared me. I could just see myself trying to fight them off if they wanted to take the clothes off my back!

I figured if I wanted to survive this place that I had better make a quick decision. I looked around the room, and I saw at least forty men! A large black man sat there looking disconsolate, but he had a kind face. I walked directly to him and said, "Unless you are here for murder, I'll make a deal with you. You keep these bums away from me, and I'll do my best to get you out of here tomorrow!"

Those were the best words he had heard since being there, and we shook hands. I needed the phone to call home. One phone, forty guys, and it was pretty tough to get in line. Not for me, my new found friend went to the first in line, "my turn next." he said and got no argument. He tapped the guy on the shoulder who was using the phone, and said "hurry." In minutes, I had the phone.

It was now about 5 PM. I called Judie

at home. Yes, the house was full of officers. They were waiting for a search warrant to arrive. One of the officers, at least, was being kind. Judie was, as always, a good hostess, serving them freshly made coffee. Yes, she did call the attorneys. They would be down to get me out as soon as possible.

I believe there was a movie entitled "The Longest Day." I know for sure now about "The Longest Night." I lived it *that* night. I found out from my attorneys later why the delay at DPS. If they had taken me straight to jail, early in the afternoon I would have attended 4:30 PM jail court. This way I had to wait until 3:30 AM.

As everyone was let out of that dirty, filthy, urine and vomit stained cell, and filed to the courtroom, I prayed I had seen the last of it!

My "protector" guarded me all night. I *was* not bothered. He had fallen on hard times. In order to leave another state with his wife and family, he overused his checking account and then left. The bank correctly thought it wasn't fair and filed charges. It cost me a little over six hundred dollars to clear the problem. I thought my cost was cheap enough considering he saved my shirt, shoes and probably my skin, which I've grown attached to (or vice versa).

I was the first called at night court, because out of some sixty people there, I was the only one to have an attorney present. Under the threat of more jail, I agreed to appear at a hearing at another court several days later, and was then released.

I scrubbed and I scrubbed and still could not seem to remove the filth from those fifteen hours of "captivity" from my body. It really did get 'under my skin' in more ways than one!

I had been released from jail at 3:30 AM, and at 10 AM the mailman brought more orders. I went to the warehouse, picked up more merchandise and was back in business!

I've told you earlier I am a tough little guy. I believe that to be true, but do not think I can't be scared. Now home from jail I discover that my motorhome is gone with all it contained, most of the clothes I owned in the world, office equipment including a leased Pitney

Bowes postage meter, notary seal, corporate seal, and *all* records accumulated since the last search and seizure, plus, worst of all, thousands and thousands of dollars worth of APRH TEA BALLS.

Chapter 24

I spent many hours during the next couple of days with my attorneys. I looked forward to the hearing. At long last, I could tell my side of the story to a judge. "Piece of cake," I wrongly, as it turned out, thought.

Judie, a good friend Jim, and myself appeared at the appointed court about ten minutes early. We sat and sat and sat. After waiting, nervously I might add, about a half an hour, *nobody* showed up, not the judge, not the DPS, not the prosecuting attorney, and *not even my attorneys!*

To say I was angry would not be correct, I was furious!!! I went to the office of the court and nobody knew anything. "Can I use your phone?" I asked. Reluctantly I was allowed. I told them I had promised under threat of more jail to be here and if necessary would set up camp and remain until I knew what was going on! I dared *not* leave for fear of penalty of not being able to prove I *was* there. Nobody, by

God, is going to jail *me* by default!

I called my attorneys from the court office. "Oh, I'm sorry, did we forget to tell you that court was postponed?" one of the junior attorneys of the firm told me.

Imagine my frustration. I had paid this firm $20,000.00 to date. I had received alot of conversation, perhaps $500.00 worth of analysis proving my innocence, and now their sorrow that they 'forgot' to tell me that there was to be no court today.

The DPS had not yet filed charges! Another date was set for early February. This time I went to the attorneys office, met them, and we went to the hearing together. The prosecution asked for a postponement, and it was granted. I found out later that the DPS had still not filed charges. Another date, and another postponement.

Each of these times, two attorneys went with me. One was $125.00 per hour, and the other $75.00 per hour. Meeting time in the office was usually 30 minutes prior to leaving plus another 15 minutes driving and parking, and an hour or so by the time we were called by the judge. Then we would drive back to the office which took fifteen minutes.

This went on perhaps ten times during February, March, and April. Hearings were scheduled for April 20, 24, and 26th. Of course, my attorneys had to be there.

For the several weeks prior to April 26th, the Prosecutor submitted many "plea agreements" to my attorneys. Each and every time I told my attorneys I would not even listen to what they said! I *demanded* a jury trial.

Unknown to me until this point, the Grand Jury had indicted me in March on five counts of possession and sale of the dangerous drug librium. I could spend fifty-six years in prison if convicted!!

At the April 24th hearing, the prosecutor and my attorneys met out of my earshot. My attorneys had been very excited that morning when I met with them at the office prior to leaving for court.

I asked what was going on. "Today you will really see us in action," the junior attorney told me. "We are filing a motion today which may put an end to the whole thing!" Now I was excited. "What is it about?" I asked. "I would rather not tell you right now." he told me.

Well, he was the attorney. I had given them $35,000.00 so I just trusted that they were looking out for my best interest.

When my attorneys rejoined me, they were all smiles. They said now they *must* insist on showing me the latest plea agreement. If I would plea 'no contest' to a couple of misdemeanors, they would give me five years probation. Guarantee me *no jail,* and fine me the value of my sports car, $2740.00.

I was furious. "You tell the prosecutor to got straight to hell. The Constitution gives me the *right* to prove my *innocence,* you know I can *do* just that."

I spoke loud enough for the prosecutor to hear me. He had been pacing the floor a short distance from us. He came over, all smiles. "Hi, Dick," he said "I really think you should let me explain this to you."

"You did all the explaining you will ever do to me the day you sat in my home questioning my daughter." I said.

135

With that he left, his face turning bright red!

I thought that this whole thing was going badly. I was told earlier that day by my attorney that *we* were in the driver's seat. I refused to further discuss any plea offer, as I had many times before.

My case was called. The prosecutor asked for postponement, and it was granted. Another $500.00 or so dollars wasted!

The hearing was re-scheduled for April 26, 1983. This was the third time in six days. The court opened, and the prosecutor asked for a recess immediately. It was granted. I was taken to the hall outside the courtroom.

Chapter 25

I just don't understand. Two weeks or so before these rushed court appearances, my attorneys, myself, and officers of the DPS made an agreement. An independent laboratory would be selected. The DPS would provide this lab with samples from the same packages they had tested. Analysis would be performed by GC/ms, absolutely the most sophisticated equipment in the world for chemical identification.

If they found the drug, I would cease business (I was selling my product everyday!). Plus I would plea that I did this "unknowingly" as I had relied on *many* lab tests reporting no drugs.

If they did *not* find the drug, the charges would be dropped. I was certainly willing to have this done. I did not believe *all* my labs could be mistaken!

Rather than use Express Mail to send the samples, Jim Welty, (officer), flew to Utah at *my* expense. That was irritating!

The lab selected was the Center for Human Toxicology in Salt Lake City. It is considered one of the best in the United States.

Their machine was under repair, so the results were not back by the 26th (court date) as expected.

My attorney took me to the end of the hall, and then proceeded to attempt to convince me to sign the latest plea agreement.

"Absolutely not, why should I?"

"Guaranteed no jail!"

"I'll not believe I'm guilty of anything until I hear it from a jury that has seen my evidence!"

"Possible fifty-five years if convicted."

"I will not plea!"

This goes on and on. At least twenty times I said no. The prosecutor storms down hearing my "no's." He literally screamed at me, "You better sign." "Go to hell!" I told him.

"I will not sign, I am going to take my

chances on the report from the lab that I am right," I told my attorney.

"If the report comes back negative you can merely withdraw," stated my attorney. Plus, you won't be in and out of court every other day."

Now *this* was beginning to make sense! "Ok, are you sure I can withdraw?" "Yes." "Are you *sure*?" "Yes."

End of court for awhile, the pressure was off! It sounded pretty good. "Ok, I'll sign but I am going to tell the judge that it is my intention to withdraw when the lab report is in." "You can not do that," my attorney told me "if you do, he will not accept it and you will still be in and out of court all the time."

"Why can't we just get a postponement until the report is in?" I asked. "The judge won't grant another postponement."

Wouldn't you know it? Ten or fifteen postponements have been granted to the prosecutor, but I can't get *one*. Justice is strange, but then what do I know.

One more time, going into the courtroom, I stop and ask my attorney if he was *sure* I could withdraw. "Of course." I was told.

Please dear reader, understand I am not very up on the law, in fact, I have *no* knowledge of it at all. When a person has paid thirty five thousand hard earned dollars to a big attorney firm you can trust their advice, can't you?

I signed!!!! The judge was happy, the prosecutor was *beaming,* and my attorney was smiling. Why did I feel so angry?

The judge asked me many, many questions. I did not feel right about this whole thing. "On my attorney's advice," to all of the questions was my answer.

The judge set the sentencing date for August 12, two and one-half months away. I didn't care, because I would have withdrawn my plea long before that!

I had to initial my "on my attorney's advice" answers for the prosecuting attorney.

"Why did you push so hard for a plea agreement?" my attorney asks him. "There was *no* way I could, with the lack of evidence take this case to a jury." replied the prosecutor!!!!

Sweeter words I have never heard. The report would come in negative. The prosecutor had stated he couldn't take the evidence he had to a jury. He certainly wouldn't be able to when the report came in negative from the Salt Lake City lab. (As you can tell I *was* confident.)

Chapter 26

Do you remember the "motion" my attorneys were so excited about? It was almost a full year before I found out the contents. It was a motion to dismiss charges stating that DPS detective Jim Welty lied many times to the Grand Jury in order to get the indictment.

My attorneys received a copy of the Grand Jury indictment in early April. The jury had convened March 13. DPS officer Welty testified; the jurors questioned him. Sounds reasonable doesn't it?

One grand juror asked, "Didn't Mr. Anderson have his product tested for librium?" "No, he did not." replied Welty. (He had a copy of every analysis I had, and they all proved negative for the drug.) *His answer was a direct lie!!!!!* One lady's husband was a customer of mine; she was *removed* as a juror!

"How much librium did Mr. Andersons product contain?" asked another juror. After being repeatedly asked *how much* it contained, Welty replied, "Our "quantitative" test proved a useable amount." *This was a direct lie.* He told the analyst not to *do* quantitative analysis. I have the report of the analyst's notes stating so, plus, the analyst admitted this in deposition!

Twenty eight times, by my count, this officer, sworn to tell the truth, *committed perjury!!!*

I can back up everything I say with official documents recording these proceeding. I do have them.

That, folks was what the motion was all about. It was filed with the court in the late afternoon on April 25th. I was convinced to sign the plea agreement early morning on the 26th.

This meant the motion would be merely thrown away. It did not have to be brought out in court. Why? Because I had signed a plea agreement making the motion *moot*!!!!

The entire case would have necessarily been thrown out of court had this motion been allowed to be acted upon in court.

I would have been a *free man*. An indictment obtained by *perjury* is absolutely, totally, and forever no good!

The entire charge against me was illegal.

Please keep in mind that I did not know this until a year later. When I was forced to become my own attorney. This is why I have copies of the official proceedings that a defendant would normally never see.

Chapter 27

During the first week of June 1983, I received a letter from my attorneys. The letter said to the effect: "Well you were right all along!"

Attached was the report from the Center for Human Toxicology in Salt Lake City, Utah

!!!NO LIBRIUM!!!

That is what it said.

375 days had passed since the problem with the DPS began. (The day Jim Welty first came to my house with Jim Treadgill!) I had not slept well any of those nights, and the days had been filled with stress.

I did not call for an appointment. I jumped in the car and drove straight to my attorney's office. I figured I had the right to be elated. The agreed upon "ultimate" authority had proven me *innocent*!!!

"Withdraw my plea" I cheerfully told Brian, the young attorney who convinced me to sign the plea.

He was not excited. I was dancing around his office, grinning from ear to ear. "Cheer up," I said. "This is one great day." Thank God the pressure was off. I was *so* happy!

"Dick, I better call Jerry in." Brian told me.

Jerry came into the office. I literally skipped over to him, shook his hand, and smilingly said, "We have finally done it, we have won. All we do is withdraw the plea and it's over!"

Jerry looked sad, and Brian had a completely dejected look on his face. I felt myself coming out of the clouds, wondering what can possibly be wrong?

"Dick," Jerry began "when Brian told you you could withdraw your plea, well it's not that easy. you see once a plea is signed it is almost impossible to withdraw."

Those words brought me closer to death emotionally than I have ever experienced. In those few minutes I went from an alltime high to the very depths of depression. "Oh God do not let this be true," I thought.

"But surely the court, when it is recognized that I am innocent, would want to see justice done." I stated.

"It doesn't work just that way" Jerry told me.

"What is the next step?" I asked.

"We better go to my office. There we can sit down, relax, and discuss your options." Jerry told me as we walked down the hallway.

"The entire firm, at our meeting this morning, upon hearing what has happened, took a vote. We have decided that Brian mis-informed you about the ability to withdraw. Therefore, you will not be billed for the expense to 'get you out of the plea.' But you must be made to realize, it is almost impossible to withdraw!"

This speech settled my nerves just a little. At least they are men enough to admit their mistake. It would not be civilized of me to be angry with them.

"We will prepare a 'Motion for Withdrawal' first." I was told. "Then the judge will decide upon it and give his decision."

I admit I left their office with mixed

emotions. I had paid them about $40,000.00 only to be told they had made a mistake whereby *I* had, on *their* advice, adjudged *myself* guilty.

Thank you God for putting me in the position of having a high tolerance for pain. I was taking full advantage of that tolerance right then!

Chapter 28

I have been called by friends 'the eternal optimist'.

That is true, especially since I have regained my health. I get kidded every once in awhile when people find out I get up *every* morning with a smile on my face; a song in my heart, and verbally say, "Good morning world."

And why not? The good Lord has given me another day of life. The sun is shining, or the rain is falling, but it really does not matter. Due to life itself, I own the world. I have another day to find happiness.

Corny, perhaps, but the day I wake up sad, unable to find *a reason* to be happy, is the day I cannot live. I cannot and will not live looking for reasons to be sad. Every single day somewhere the birds are singing, a babe is born, someone will give you a smile, pat you on the back, or tell you they love you. Do not ever let a day go by that you do not give someone a smile. Both lives will be infinitely richer for it, and the best part is that *IT'S FREE!!!*

A 'petition for evidentiary hearing' was prepared and filed with the court in July 1983. Several days later I received word that the petition was 'granted'. The hearing was scheduled for August 3rd. Finally after all this time and perhaps thirty hearings, the very first words spoken in my defense would be heard.

The prosecutor began getting very friendly with my attorneys; he even tried to be 'friends' with me. I was suspicious. He said, "How terribly expensive all this will be for you, expert witness fees, one flying in from Salt Lake City and all. Perhaps I can help. I'll draw up a better plea agreement!"

I'm afraid I did not take kindly to this approach. Do you remember earlier, the day I signed the plea, he told my attorney and myself he "could not" take his case to a jury for lack of evidence? Well I *wanted* a trial by jury to present *my* evidence. That is what this hearing was for, so I could withdraw the plea and have a jury trial. I felt confident that no one could prevent me having my trial now.

New and better pleas were brought by the prosecutor. I would not listen!! I did not want a plea to begin with; I certainly didn't want one now. So many were offered that I finally got tired and sent back a note written on toilet paper suggesting what he might do with his pleas. *I DIDN'T WANT ONE.*

I was *happy* to pay for this. Once the expert witnesses have testified they are not able to detect drugs in my product, the judge will *have* to allow me to withdraw my plea and go to trial. This is my constitutional right. Right?

Chapter 29

All was arranged. My expert witness from the Human Toxicology Laboratory was here from Salt Lake City. Mr. Bolin represents his laboratory. Both of my attorneys are in court, and of course, so am I.

The State of Arizona had the analysts from the DPS Lab and analysts from the FDA Lab in Los Angeles.

As quickly as court came into session, the judge makes a statement. "I do not have time to hear this case today, recessed until 10 AM tomorrow."

I could have died. This had been set up for about one month. My cost was in the thousands. Every hour, whether or not court was held, I had to pay the Ph.D from Salt Lake, plus his room and board at one of Phoenix's finest, plus now an auto rental.

The State, of course, had to spend taxpayer's money doing the same for their witness.

I was upset, but my attorney's had

the correct answer, "These things happen."

Me nervous? Mr. Confidence? Why 110 beats a minute is normal. Hands and entire body quivering are normal, right?

Court convened. I heard every word. Each one seemed magnified. This was, after all, the *first* day of the rest of my life!

I just glowed. my expert witnesses testified that *no librium* was detected in my APRH TEA BALLS.

Now I know, no matter what the opposition says, there would be *reasonable doubt* of guilt. Of course I forgot that reasonable doubt is *only* valid in a jury trial.

The State analysts said they found librium. I certainly expected that.

One of the FDA analysts confirmed, "Yes, we found librium," then added "we also found Indomethacin and Hydrochlorothiazide!"

That did not surprise me. Actually, I expected them to name about nine drugs as listed in various newspaper articles.

"Did you find librium each and every

time you analyzed the APRH TEA BALLS?" my attorney asked him.

"Yes."

"You never tested any samples that did *not* contain librium?"

"No, they all contained librium."

"You are absolutely sure?"

"Yes, I'm sure."

My mind was screaming, *PERJURY.* I knew what was coming. I had seen their analysis!

My attorney held up a sheet of paper, "Do you recognize this?"

"I can't see it from here."

I was *so* proud of my attorney at this minute. This was better than Perry Mason!

"Let me read part of it to you, 'NO LIBRIUM FOUND', your name is signed on the bottom as the analyst."

"Do you remember it now?"

"Yes."

"Why did you just say you *always* found librium in APRH TEA BALLS?"

"I forgot."

"You mean something as important as this to Mr. Anderson's case, you forgot?"

"I forgot."

Chapter 30

Sleepless nights. I could write a book about the subject concerning the three nights following that hearing.

Carpet wearing due to pacing? My carpet will never be the same, after suffering the punishment I gave it during those days.

Finally, on the fourth day, a letter from my attorney arrived. This is it. I paced some more. "Open it!" Judie insisted.

I was relishing the feeling of elation soon to be experienced upon learning that I could finally have my trial to prove my innocence!

I opened it.

"Dear Dick," it started. (my attorneys and I had been on a first name basis for a long time). "The judge has decided he will not allow you to withdraw your plea. He gives no reason as it is not necessary, you see this sort of thing is 'discretionary of the court.'"

Do you know the feeling you get when someone close to you has died? One's heart seems to inflate, it is difficult to breathe, and there is terrible pain! Yes, I am tough but not so tough. I broke down and cried.

August 12, 1983 was one of the hardest days of my life. I had to go in front of the Superior Court Judge to be sentenced as a criminal.

I insisted on paying my attorneys through the past proceedings. Anyone can make a mistake! Jerry and I met before the sentencing hearing. He again stated the firm would not charge me for further work to 'get me out' of the plea. I was in no mood to be happy even with this good news.

The court convened, and then the judge made the necessary remarks. He then asked me if I had anything to say?

Oh yes, I had *never* been given an opportunity to speak in my own defense, and oh yes, I had something to say.

I had prepared a little speech waiting for this opportunity.

I walked up and stood before the bench, then turned slightly so everyone present would be sure to hear me. At the risk of being redundant with information previously stated, I would like you to know, word for word what I said to the court that day.

"I stand before this court today to be sentenced as a criminal. I think it is only fair that the court be aware that I am still to this day in the same business that is the reason for my being here. The only difference now is that my accusers, the DPS, now say, 'good luck in your business' we are not going to bother you any more.' This is my product, APRH TEA BALLS," I said, holding a package of product up for all to see. "After thirty-six months of persecution and prosecution my attorneys say I *might* be given five or ten minutes to speak in a court of law on my own behalf. It is ironic. Drugs are what *I* am most fearful of. I have many customers and friends whose whole bodies are ravaged beyond belief by the side and after effects of drugs approved as *safe and effective.*"

"I am arthritic. Twenty- one years ago, my feet began swelling, my ankles were immobile, and calcium built up on my heel. I walked with a cane. Special shoes were ordered, and cortisone was injected. After a year of being treated by four physicians I was worse. Surgery removed bone from my right heel. The surgeon told me I would be a cripple in a few years!

I moved my family to Arizona for the dry heat. I feel that it helped or slowed down the degeneration. However, I have had two more surgeries for arthritis since living here. I have been attended to by approximately twenty doctors in Arizona. Prescriptions for Indocin, Clinerol, Butazoladin alka and a host of other drugs were prescribed to me. Cortisone was injected into my joints. *All drugs* had one effect: I became *worse.*

In September 1979 I awoke, unable to get out of bed. My entire body was wracked with pain. The pain suffered by arthritics *cannot* be described verbally. I suggest to the court to look into the eyes of an arthritic, *then* you can see the suffering!

For eight months, September '79 through May 5th '80 I suffered. Four doctors did their best to make my life endurable with a singular result: I became worse and worse. Several times during that period, I went to bed with a loaded gun vowing not to spend another night in pain.

My disease had cost myself approximately $75,000.00 to date. In desperation, I tried every home remedy I heard of.

I know that miracles are scoffed at even though our country says "In God we trust" and "God bless America", they are hollow phrases. But my standing in front of this court today, physically fit, able to walk upright as a normal human being is a *miracle* thanks to Chinese wisdom in using herbs as medicine. The bible says, "The tree shall bear fruit for your food, and the herb thereof to cure your sickness." In my case, I know I will never be cured, but by feeding my body what it requires to combat arthritis, I can live a normal life.

I entered into this plea agreement on the advice of my attorney with the *understanding that I and I alone* could re-open the case. Not until after the fact did I know about the 'new evidence' provision.

Now after having samples from each and every shipment analyzed using a total of about fifteen laboratories nationwide to prove the absence of drugs, I find that I have, by virtue of the plea agreement adjudged *myself* a criminal.

The State laboratories of several states plus FDA registered and FDA certified labs have found no drug in my product. Yet David Rubin and James Welty, the county attorney and the DPS officer, have vowed to put me out of business. I wish to go on record with the statement, 'I have not yet begun to fight'.

People buy my product of their own free will. It does not make them drunk, it does not make them high, it does not depress them, it does not put them to sleep, it does not wake them up, it does not put their life in danger, and it does not put their neighbor's lives in danger. It *does* relieve pain and suffering incomprehensible to a normal person. There are 31,600,000 arthritics in this country, and if our right to use a product natural to God's green earth is a crime then I am a criminal. My only desire is that I be given the *right* to present my case to a jury of my peers and let *them* make the decision!

I request that my belongings, all of them, be returned to myself. I request that clothing, linens and tools be replaced that were ruined by a leaking roof at the DPS warehouse where they were stored and the motorcycle that was 'sold' be replaced and that all my records, merchandise, checks, contracts, testimonials and letters be returned *now!*

Chapter 31

The next one year (almost to the day) was so filled with legal set-backs, heart-aches and sorrow I cannot bear reliving it as I write this, so briefly:

I was sentenced to three years probation. I was not allowed to possess my guns, and I could not sell any product which contained drugs or was sold for a therapeutic purpose. I was given 120 hours of community service work and about ten other little details. Oh, one of the big ones was that I could not travel outside of the State of Arizona without first obtaining a travel permit from my probation officer!

Upon leaving the courtroom my attorney escorted me to the probation department. Now I was alone!

I told the interviewer, "When I leave here I am going home to fill today's orders with the very same product that has put me in front of you today. If that is illegal I should be arrested now for breaking probation!"

It was a scary thing to do, but I refused to lie. He wrote this into the report but declined to take action. I told him I, to operate my business had to go frequently to California. He gave me a 'travel permit' to legally do this. He then assigned a probation officer and told me on threat of immediate arrest, "do not fail to make an appointment to see her by tomorrow."

Well I'm only a little bit stupid. I am willing to go to jail to accomplish my goal to make my product recognized as legal, but I won't go to jail on a legal technicality.

I had one chance in Superior Court called a review due to new evidence. Brian prepared the "ineffective assistance of counsel" case again himself. He asked me to find another law firm to represent me as he could not due to conflict of interest. I asked an acquaintance of mine, Stewart, who is a good attorney, if he would represent me. He agreed, but told me criminal cases were not his field. Since he did not have to prepare the case, only present it in court that which Brian had prepared, I was satisfied he could do the job.

The chief lawyer had quit the firm. I

was invited in to meet the new one who would be taking over my case. I asked about the 'free' part of the deal, and there was some stammering. I said, "if the offer was not made in good faith, I will pay my bill in full this minute."

"Oh no, it was made in good faith, we just have not figured exactly how to handle it" is pretty close to what Jerry told me that day.

Brian testified to the court, to the same judge as before that he did in fact provide 'ineffective assistance of counsel'. The Judge's reaction literally taken was "signing is signing, Mr. Anderson signed so I am holding him to it."

By this time, I don't even get rattled. I know in my heart this judge was somehow so prejudiced against me nothing would penetrate!

Chapter 32

I realize that I perhaps sound over critical of the law firm that convinced me to sign the plea agreement. I finally fired them because:

1. The "new" lawyer I had discovered had been a judge. In that position, he had signed some of the search warrants 'against me'.
2. I had been told that I would not be billed for their time to get me out of the plea agreement. Over a six month period I asked many times where I stood with them monetarily, receiving no answer. Then I received a bill in the mail with a "dead beat" letter.

I do have copies of the letters going back and forth. They eventually threatened lawsuit if I did not pay the more than $5,000.00 bill. Months later, after retaining a new law firm I asked what I might do. They suggested I negotiate. I did, and then I paid $3,000.00 in return for a receipt 'paid in full'.

At this point I had no one to fight for me. The original firm had, thank God, timely filed for an appeal to get me out of the signing of the plea agreement. At least they did one thing right.

During the next three weeks I called or met with about twenty different attorneys searching for someone to represent me in the Court of Appeals to no avail. The two main reasons were; lack of expertise in appeals and, though unspoken, an unwillingness to "fight against a fellow lawyer."

I then talked to Stewart, he said, "I know a very good attorney, though expensive, who *would* take your case to the appeals court." I *was* appreciative.

Stewart had my entire file sent to his friend.

I had never met this new attorney. He called me the day he received my file. "If a petition for review is not filed by 5

PM tonight, you will lose forever your right to do so.'' were his first words to me.

I must be a quick study, as I no doubt hold the world record for going to law school and graduating in two hours.

No, he could not get to it, but he was willing to tell me on the phone the principle. I grabbed my legal pad of notes, jumped into my car, and drove to the downtown courthouse. At 3:30 PM I was standing in line where the filing takes place. Ten or so people were in front of me. The clock is running. At 4 PM, I'm in front of the line. ''You have got to be joking,'' the young man tells me, ''I have no idea of how you draw up a petition, I'm a clerk. Go see 'so and so' on the third floor.

I went to see the person referred to. ''Can't help.'' I was sent to see someone else. ''Can't help,'' I was sent to another place, no help!

I'm not ashamed to tell you tears were welling as I found myself back at the 'filing' room at 4:30 with nothing accomplished. ''I *won't* be beat'' I thought so I took my legal pad, and to the best of my ability, handwrote with carbon

taken from a waste basket, so I would
have a copy of the world's worst 'petition for relief.' I was the last in line. At 5
PM sharp, the young man stamped "filed" on my copy. *I had protected my
right!!!!*

Chapter 33

I had an appointment to meet my "new" attorney at 6 PM the following evening. As is my practice, I was on time.

Wow, this guy took your breath away. He 'ain't' big, (shorter than I) but he had a reputation for being 'tough as nails'.

"I think I can win your appeal, of course there are no guarantees, here is how it will work. You give me $30,000.00, then I don't want to see you again. I work entirely on my own. When it's over you'll know if you won or lost!"

Like I said, "WOW." My mind raced to all the attorneys I had dealt with in the past. You know what, I'm not able to count them among my best friends. Please don't get me wrong, I sincerely believe that attorneys are just as fine a group of people as anyone. In fact, I am not mad at and certainly do not *dislike* the attorneys I had just been associated with. It's just that circumstances, of my own doing, have put me in front of this particular attorney. Unfortunately they have been necessary in my life during the last few years.

I did not have $30,000.00 at the moment and even if I did would not have given it to him, 'just like that'. I offered to give him $5,000.00 to start. He replied, "cash now or no deal". He just got fired!!!!

Chapter 34

Well folks, meet the first self-accredited, died in the wool, gung-ho, dumb as you please attorney, yep, ya guessed, it's me.

There is a saying, "The man who acts as his own attorney has a fool for a client." There is another saying, "If you want a job done right, do it yourself."

I don't know about doing it right, but I'll guarantee no attorney *ever* worked harder or believed his client's innocence more than *this* attorney.

Three solid months, day after day, I crammed, studied and read law books, called the Arizona State Statutes.

I filed with the Appeals Court Motions and Petitions one after the other. A motion to extend time, so I would have more time to prepare my case (denied). A motion for legal assistance (denied). A motion to consolidate "Petition for Review, and "Appeal". (Granted) A motion to dismiss, when the State failed to timely respond to another motion. (Denied). Petition to recognize me as ''attorney.'' (Granted).

Finally, the last document was filed. The "Opening Brief." I had done my best.

Chapter 35

Judie and I got on a plane and went to Kansas to see my sister and brother whom I had not seen in years.

YES,
FIRST I GOT MY TRAVEL PERMIT!!

Seeing my brother and his family and my sister and hers, what a time we had. We sang the same old songs we did as kids. Of course, then Dad sang with us. He went to his reward many years ago but old softy me, seeing at least part of the family together again touched me deeply enough that it showed a couple of times. Ah, who wants to hear about that.

My brother's son taught me to 'break dance', I ran foot races, and I might mention ate too much. Necessarily, I cannot name all those family members who brought me so much pleasure. I hope they realize I love them all.

Judie and I returned home on the 12th of August. I was so enthralled by my brother's magical fingers on the banjo, that I went right out and bought two of them.

Two days later, there was a knock on my door. I answered it. "Hello," I said, (normal reaction, right?) "can I help you?"

"I am a Federal Marshall here to serve papers on you." the man told me. No, he's not kidding!

Do you know how many sheets of paper it takes to make a stack of about five inches? I don't either, but let me tell you it's a bunch.

When he left, I looked at Judie and said, "Well, I've been just too lucky, sooner or later it was bound to happen. I guess maybe they've got me this time. I can't fight the U.S. Government."

The first thing I thought of is jail. "Here I go," I thought. "Wait a minute this says 'civil', let me see?"

I began reading. Thinking to myself "not so bad this, not so bad that."

I got cocky again, "You know," I told Judie, "this may be beatable."

I went right to work. Remember I'm my own hot-shot attorney these days. I'm ready to go back to the law books and start filing motions, petitions, etc. Please realize I didn't know my butt from a hole in the ground but I couldn't just say "I quit!" Or at least I wouldn't!

Then as the good Lord would have it, I was referred to a man who is now a consultant, believe it or not, to people just like me.

Owen agreed to come to my office (in my home) and discuss the problem with me. I bared my soul as to what had transpired with the state case and now this. Well Owen, with his twenty years experience working *for* the FDA knew and told me that this was not something I could do by myself.

I told him of my inability to find an attorney to work with me. "Would you like for me to find one for you?" Owen asked. I said, "Yes."

A couple of days later Jay Geller called me from Los Angeles. "Send me a copy of everything." Oh yes I'll do that. A small retainer went with it. The only thing I insisted upon was that I wanted a copy of every paper that went to the court. If I cannot be totally informed, I wouldn't hire him.

What, this is his procedure? He wants me to be informed? Already we were starting off on good ground.

Listen to this; Jay is licensed in California. The court that has jurisdiction is in Arizona. To practice here, he must hire a local firm to work with him. He informs me their name is Levy, Sherwood, Klien and Dudley, P.A. The only thing I don't like about them is the "looong" name when I write them a check. Other than that, they have proven themselves to be, along with Jay, the best thing that could have happened. I look at it this way, somebody upstairs is looking down on me. I *must* be doing something right!

Chapter 36

If you're as tired of reading this crap as I am of typing it, bear with me. I'm shifting into high gear now.

In November 1983, Leung Lo, my herbal advisor from Chinatown L.A., and I flew to Hong Kong. We did not go there to ride a sampan but to accomplish something that was impossible to do in the United States.

My desire was to make an attempt at buying the formulating process of the herbs so I could duplicate the effect of the APRH TEA BALLS from raw herbs in the United States. There is *no* problem in importing the raw herbs. Then I would be in the position to manufacture the *best* product in the world to help arthritis, and do it completely under the auspices of the FDA.

I am a good salesman, (I'm also modest but it is true) however, they would not sell me the formula. They *did* offer a trade. If I could give them the Coca Cola formula they would give me their formula.

Oh well, I tried.

YES, I HAD GOTTEN A TRAVEL PERMIT!

Jay was working on the case. I was developing a new product. I named it EARTH'S MAGIC. I wrote a letter to all of my customers. "No more APRH TEA BALLS, new tablet, new name, new color, new label, new manufacturer, new company name." (original too long like the attorneys).

The old product was out on the 12th of October; in with the new on the 15th of October.

We were scheduled for federal court hearing October 22, 1984. Jay flew into Phoenix and I met him face to face for the first time. We met at the local attorneys office, and we walked to court from there.

Court convened. The FDA asked for a recess, and I was taken into a little room. Jay talked to the FDA prosecutor who flew in from Washington D.C. to handle the case for the FDA. Jay came into the little room and said, "Dick, if you sign this it's all over." Well nothing is that easy. Remember, I'm pretty shy about signing my name to *anything* legal anymore; a fox is pretty skittish after being in that first trap!

I came geared mentally for a fight. It was kind of like being in the ring and nothing but air to swing at. I ranted, I raved, I stormed about, I probably kicked the wall, but I don't remember for sure.

Finally Jay said, "If you sign this paper you can go home and fill your orders, just that easy. All you're signing is that you won't sell black pills, round pills, APRH TEA BALLS, or any product named in the charges. You also cannot sell any pills containing drugs, since you have laboratory reports showing no drugs in your product and you believe there is none in EARTH'S MAGIC the whole thing is over."

Once I settled down and read the document, I realized he was right. I signed, still in business. All finished with the case. "Whew."

Somebody in the FDA does not like me. How do I know? Easy, they wrote a letter to the DPS saying I sold drugs while on probation. Although not true, Indomethacin and Hydrochlorothiazide were the FDA's accusations in their letter concerning APRH TEA BALLS.

Chapter 37

A knock came on our back door. I believe it's the first time anyone ever came to the back. It was my neighbor, "Dick, there is a car sitting down at the corner, I think it is plain clothes officers." He had the license number of the vehicle.

I had had a call from Brian (attorney from the first firm) yesterday. He had informed me that there was a warrant out for my arrest. How did he know?

Upon hearing that, I went directly to my new found local attorneys, (long name). They called the probation officer. She said, "under the circumstances I will quash the warrant."

I did not trust the officials however, so I stayed at home this morning rather than go out to breakfast. I refused to give them an opportunity to stop me in my new car, arrest me, and seize it.

Well they got tired of waiting for me to leave and about fifteen minutes later they were at the door. "You are under arrest for probation violation." said Jim Welty (DPS officer) "What is the charge?" I had the presence of mind to ask. "Possession and sales of drugs while on probation." I was told. "You're quite mistaken," I said (I've tried this before with no success) "Let me show you my analysis." "Your analysis are no good." Oh well, I tried.

Have you ever played monopoly? You know, go straight to jail?

Guess where they took me? Straight to jail. I was not too upset. I had played this game before.

My attorney came down; they let me out of the cell and let me sit in a little room to talk. He stayed until afternoon court. I was first called as my attorney was present. "Probation violation, no bail." the judge said.

Fear. Do you really know what that word means? I must confess it took on new meaning for me at that moment. I am not going to explain further as it could not help this story.

All I can and will say is that

something good 'oft comes from something seemingly unbearable.

While here for twenty-eight days in this dirty, rotten, stinking, hellhole, God-forsaken place, I decided to and did write the rough draft of this book.

You know, if a person robs, steals, murders, and is not a nice guy generally twenty -eight days may be cheap payment. To me it was a LIFETIME. I get out today!

Chapter 38

I suppose I should tell you how I got out of jail. First of all no charges *were ever filed!* I bet some of you will say "but that's not legal."

I paid $20,000.00 in retainers while I was there. I would have paid a million (if I had it). My attorney from California flew over and worked with the local attorneys. Exactly what happened, I don't know. The state did decide they could not *possibly* prove drug charges and *that's why* charges were not filed. God forbid, if they were filed they might be forced into letting me have a jury trial. Well, we all know by now they *will not* allow that!

Whoops, the state has a problem. They kept me in jail for twenty-eight days. We all know that in this great country (I really do mean that) a person cannot be thrown and kept in jail for no reason? What they really *needed* now was a reason. They can't even let me go until they have one.

They did, of course, confiscate everything in sight the day they arrested me. Funny though, they only took about 100 bottles of EARTH'S MAGIC. They left thousands more sitting right where they were. But they cleaned out my file cabinet of *all* records. It's a shame, I guess, that they have gone over and over my records for the last few years and just can't seem to find anything wrong. I pay my taxes, dumb me even ahead of time, I pay my bills, my credit is A-1, I have *no* customer complaints, everything is in order. I suppose the above sounds like bragging. Really I'm not, I do run a tight ship as we said in the Navy, and I'm proud of it.

Well, are you convinced I am a good guy? I hate to burst the bubble, but now I must tell you, yes, I guess I am a criminal after all. Have you noticed how I wrote in caps, THAT I ALWAYS GOT THE NEEDED TRAVEL PERMITS. Do you remember?

I was first given a travel permit for the STATE of California but it was temporary. The permanent replacement said Los Angeles and San Diego. I had to travel to these cities frequently for my business, and of course they wouldn't want to jeopardize my business of selling pills. Hold everything, something is crazy here! Why do they give me travel permits to do the business that they have vowed to put me out of? Someday I'll have to ask these nice officers to explain it. I know that they are smarter than me.

Have I got your attention? Listen close now.

One day I flew to L.A., rented a car, took care of business, and drove to Santa Barbara to visit a friend in the hospital. He had just gone through back surgery and was still getting around in a wheel chair. The doctors let him go out to dinner with me. Of course, I promised to take good care of him. We had a fine dinner at a restaurant on a pier. I paid with my credit card so I would have a receipt. You see he is a customer as well as a friend.

There you see, I am a criminal!

I didn't get a travel permit to leave the L.A. area!

This was not the justice I was taught, but what do I know?

The state was good about it though, if I would plead guilty to the charge of probation violation they would not file drug charges and would drop the remaining two thirds of my probation. What? Sign another plea agreement?

You bet!

Chapter 39

Have I told you my local attorneys are good? Well, they are great! They have taken an interest in my case. They called one day to tell me they had discussed taking the state case all the way to the Supreme Court.

Do you remember I told you I became my own attorney? Of course I am not an attorney, but I did my best. I lost the appeal that I worked so hard on. Three judges studied the case, two voted against me. One however, voted *for* me, very strongly. He wrote a lengthy explanation as to why he did. I never feel real bad if I lose anything as long as I performed to the best of my ability.

"We feel pretty confident you can prevail if you hire us to take the case to the Supreme Court of Arizona, you do not have to give us a retainer. We will bill you at the end of each month." said Tom, the attorney who would be preparing the Supreme Court case.

"WRONG MUST FAIL, RIGHT PREVAIL."

I hope the customer who wrote me these words of confidence reads this book. I want her to know I have taken them to heart, and they have kept me going. (The DPS seized her letter along with hundreds like it four years ago. They have not yet been returned. I can't remember her name.)

"Yes, go to work." I told him.

Time passes. Of course, nothing with the legal system goes quickly. But I am more relaxed than I have been for a long time. What will be will be.

The Supreme Court of Arizona ruled unanimously in my favor!!! Brian was *wrong* for convincing me to sign the plea agreement. The DPS Lab *did not* find any amount of librium in the product. In every respect they had found that I had not received *justice* by the Superior Court.

They remanded it back to the Superior Court for trial, (trial, finally?) The Superior Court upon receiving this order from the Supreme Court overturned the indictment, knowing that they had no case. You remember, thats the one where Jim Welty, the DPS officer committed perjury, this fact is now recognized by the Supreme Court.

The Superior Court now admits that I *was* innocent all along. You remember the little MG sports car I was driving the first time I was arrested? They evaluated that car at $2740.00. Then they fined me that amount the day I was sentenced.It was so nice of them. Since I was not guilty of a crime, they will pay me back the money. That was ruled by the court April 4, 1986.

The poor state, their records are not as good as mine. They have lost track of what they did with my car or the proceeds from the sale thereof. Now it is three months later, and I'm still not paid. It's funny, if I don't pay my sales tax on time (which I do) I get penalties and interest, and even jail if I cheat. Well, we know they won't cheat me.

I asked my attorney "how I should go about getting back *all* of the items confiscated with the four illegal search warrants?" He suggested the first thing would be for me to make a formal request by letter. I did. I sent them a bill for $339,000.00 about a month ago. It's pretty close to accurate but impossible to be sure. Each time they would come with a search warrant they would seize the record of what they had seized the time before. Oh well, I suppose that is how the law works. What do I know?

The next step would be to file lawsuit against the officers. But the state has immunity. I can't sue them. Oh well, I suppose that is the way it is. After all, I'm only a citizen who has been found innocent by the highest court. Why shouldn't I have to suffer the loss. By the way, how much is twenty-eight days loss of freedom worth. Oh not much I guess, after all I'm only a citizen of the greatest country on earth. What could *one* be worth? There are too many to worry about, and we can't concern ourselves over one.

Chapter 40

I have no quarrel concerning the value of a regulatory agency such as the FDA. They are, after all, the watch-dog over the public's health and well-being.

One thing that troubles me is that the inspector from the Phoenix office told me just recently that the number one job of the FDA is to follow through and check out consumer complaints. I asked him, "How many complaints have you had concerning me or my product?" His answer was, "To the best of my knowledge, not a single one." "Why has the FDA spent hundreds of thousands of taxpayer's dollars giving me problems over a product that brings no complaints?" I asked. His answer was simply, "I do not know."

If no one gets sick, if no one dies, if I am not making untrue claims, if many, many laboratories find *no* drugs in the product, what can possibly be so bad about it?

The other side of the coin is that almost 100% of the four thousand plus people that use it or have used it report good to fantastic benefits. From a humanitarian standpoint, should it not be allowed to be used of one's own free will?

I am going to suggest some possible answers.

The cost to arthritic's for medical fees, drugs, therapies, artificial joints, etc. is about $15,000,000,000.00 equals 15 *billion* a year. Fifteen billion dollars is an easier way to say it but looking at the numbers may help to visualize the point I am going to make. A high price considering that *nothing* the medical profession has at it's disposal today does very much to *reduce* the suffering of the arthritic. Elimination of pain is just a fantasy, medically speaking. It is indeed sad.

Suppose for a moment that a product were all of a sudden available which would eliminate the need for many drugs, office calls, therapies, and artificial joints. How happy would the huge drug corporations be if their drugs were no longer needed? Do you suppose any of the money taken in by these corporations finds its way into the political arena? Are we totally naive?

Now then suppose 40,000,000 *votes* were put into play? Would that wield some power? At the end of this book you will be given an opportunity to *FIGHT BACK*. Of course it will cost some money, 22 cents and an envelope. Would you help me? I am trying to help you, but I cannot do it alone.

We arthritics, if we banded together, could become an awesome force.

Individually we are weak of body, and let us not kid ourselves, we eventually in our pain, necessarily become too weak to *FIGHT BACK*. Many hundreds of thousands of arthritics have been ruined financially, unable to work. Mothers are unable to take care of their children. I *know* I've been there!

You just read of the miracle that happened to me. I wish you could read the more than 1,000 letters from customers with the same story. I have received seventy more in the past three weeks. They would make you cry for happy!

The only way I have had the strength to fight is because once my body became whole, my mind became whole, and I became so strong that I have taken on some huge forces and prevailed, so far.

Chapter 41

I am under seige again! On May 23rd, 1986, that's forty-three days ago today, a knock came on my door. "Why hello Mr. Shea, how are you?" I asked. Mr. Shea is the local FDA investigator. We have known each other just lacking four years. He was with the DPS on August 25, 1982 on the first search warrant.

He was the *only* person that day who was a gentleman. He took me aside and made it very clear he was there as an observer only and pointed out he had nothing whatsoever to do with the warrant.

More than that, we have met many times in the line of his duty inspecting my premises. When I made the agreement with the FDA not to sell round pills, black pills, etc. they wrote into the agreement much stronger powers than they are normally afforded under the law. I didn't care because I had nothing to hide.

He treated me with respect and I did likewise. Under other circumstances, we could be friends. All I am saying is that he is a nice man. That day he acted downcast, as if he did not like what he had to do. Strange, I tried to put *him* at ease. I knew he had a job to do. "Mr. Anderson, this is a Federal Marshall, we have a warrant to serve." Those were not the 'sweetest' words I've ever heard. Oh well. "Please come into my office," I said. Once in and seated the marshall handed me the papers. I glance at them, sure enough, 'warrant for arrest' is exactly what it said. "May I call my attorney before you take me away?" I ask. "Oh you are not under arrest, only two lot numbers of EARTH'S MAGIC," Mr. Shea quickly told me.

Whew!!

All they did was put a Federal notice on the boxes (3971 bottles) that they could not be moved under penalty of law.

I am effectively, but temporarily, out of business again. I quickly typed a newsletter, had it printed, and put it in the mail to customers, informing them of current harrassment, and of the fact that there might be a slight, unavoidable delay in filling orders.

Remember, this all started with a newspaper article December 16, 1980. They claimed then my product contained six drugs and two toxins! At least now I've got them down to one, Indomethacin!

Have any of my products ever contained Indomethacin?

The following report was received by a customer from the Health Department, Public Health Center, 250 So. 4th St. Minneapolis, Minnesota 55415. David M. Lurie, Commissioner of Health.

September 22, 1982

Mrs. P. McLain
Traverse City, Michigan 49684

Dear Mrs. McLain
Sample No. 8486 submitted for analysis was reported on September 16, 1982 by our Street Drug Analysis Lab as:
suspect Indomethacin, not confirmed
Several similar samples with the same alleged contents were examined by the F.D.A. They only confirm

our findings: suspect Indomethacin-not confirmed

Sincerely,
Bruce Taylor
Project Coordinator
Street Drug Analysis

Exactly thirty days following the date on this report I faced the FDA in Federal Court charged with Indomethacin. The FDA Lab in Detroit, Michigan (see report) *agreed* with *all* my laboratories yet I was forced to spend tens of thousands of dollars in legal fees plus agree to *never* sell that product again because they said the product *did* contain Indomethacin.

So many questions need to be answered. I shutter to think it could possibly be me and *all* the laboratories that say *no drugs* are wrong. Logically, we are not.

By getting answers from official agencies for the following questions we could perhaps all sleep better.

Six drugs plus two toxins were originally charged in the newspaper article.

1. Why have the charges of five drugs

and both toxins dropped?

2. Did state and FDA laboratories make mistakes?

The product was called a potential killer.

3. Where are the dead or sick people caused by using the product?

4. Why do almost 100% of the people who use the product find relief from suffering?

5. Why have I not been taken to trial?

6. Why have I not been legally forced to stop distributing EARTH'S MAGIC if they are right?

Chapter 42

As you can probably tell in reading this I have a certain amount of pent up anger. I have thought of a way to release the pressure I have suffered from this feeling. In my mind I am charging the FDA with *ATTEMPT* to cover up the truth concerning my product, EARTH'S MAGIC which I believe to be potentially beneficial to millions of United States citizen's.

I have over the years been summoned to appear before many courts and now as a citizen of these United States I wish I could serve the following summons on the FDA.

You are hereby served this summons, under penalty of public scrutiny, to face me publicly, to hold national court.

You will bring your witnesses, all of them, the best you can muster, and your very best defense lawyer to speak in your behalf.

I am the prosecutor, and will bring my real experts, the users of EARTH'S MAGIC. My laboratory analysts, the M.D.'s, the D.O.'s, the Rheumatologists, clinicians, researchers and cancer clinic directors.

COME PREPARED

This is the championship fight and we do want to give the audience their moneys worth.

AND SO SPEAKETH THE LAW!

That folks is how the *cow* ate the cabbage.
Now I feel better!
THE END

Epilogue

Laws are made to be challenged and changed or amended for the betterment of society.

I believe my case was and is:

Too big for James Welty, Sgt. Stocksdale and Mike Taylor to investigate.

Too big for David Rubin to prosecute.

Too big for Judge Cantor to pass sentence.

Too big for the FDA.

Too big for only twelve jurors to decide.

I would like to think my customers and I could ask the citizens and the arthritics of this great country to join us in our FIGHT BACK!

We are the public, we are the law and all we ask is justice.

The ball is in your court.

If you would like to join this fight sign the letter on the last page and get it mailed!

You may save my skin and as I said earlier I have become attached to it. (Or is it the other way around?)

THE FOLLOWING ARE JUST A FEW OF THE TYPICAL LETTERS RECEIVED

Dear Mr. Anderson,

I have suffered from rheumatoid arthritis since 1971. Treatment included large doses of aspirin, every anti-inflammatory drug on the market, gold therapy, plaquenil, and surgery for joint replacement.

All of the above-mentioned drugs caused serious stomach problems and complicated my existing problems. I reached the point where I became so hypersensitive that I could not tolerate any of them.

I have been taking your product, "Earth's Magic" for 15 months and I'm happy to say I have not experienced any side effects. I feel like a new person. My arthritis has improved and I can now participate in life and living.

I don't know what I would do without Earth's Magic.

Sincerely,
V. Beiles

To Whom It May Concern:

We have been using EARTH'S MAGIC for the past seven years and wish to say we would very much dislike having to be without it under any circumstances.

My husband takes six tablets a day and it keeps him out of pain and helps him through a days work. He has tried to do without the tablets but finds that the pain comes back very soon and he is always very uncomfortable. Then when he starts again it will take twelve tablets a day for the first week then he can go back to six tablets a day. There have been no side effects and we do not believe there are any drugs in these tablets. In our opinion the medical profession will prescribe much stronger drugs for the same purpose and some of these will have side effects. It seems to us that the medical profession is just unhappy because there is something on the market to help people and it is cutting into their pockets because, after taking the tablets, people don't need their prescriptions or make office visits which are very costly.

We appreciate the concern of the FDA for our well being but if we do not keep the EARTH'S MAGIC then we feel they really do not care about the general public but only where the money is coming from to get this product off the market.

We stand behind EARTH'S MAGIC 100%

Sincerely,
Mrs. W. E. Price
Texas

Dear Mr. Anderson,

I am surprised and disgusted that you have to go to court again. I really can't understand why anyone would want you to stop making Earth's Magic.

Soon I will be sixty-five. Recently I went in for a physical examination from a practicing M.D. and he was very pleased at my physical and mental condition. I have never felt better than I do now.

After years of pain and disability I am now teaching Church School, substituting in the public schools, doing all my own housework, walking four miles a day and making use of all the pain free time with joy. It is so nice to feel good.

Have these people that are trying to make you stop making your herbs ever had arthritis???? If they had and had tried all the remedies available they would surely leave you alone and let us enjoy our good health....

I certainly don't want to run out of herbs. I have a time or two and found out what it was like before I started taking them. I don't believe your herbs will cure my arthritis but they surely make each day pain free as long as I take them. Thanks for sharing them with me and my neighbors.

I started taking your herbs at least four years ago and each time I go in for a physical (which is about once a year) my doctor is pleased with my almost perfect health. It seems to be improving each year. I certainly hope you can continue making Earth's Magic—I would hate to even think about going back to aspirin, mental dullness and pain.

Sincerely,
V. B. Doughten
Montana

Dear Sir,

I have used "Earth's Magic" for my arthritis about two years now and find it the best help to stop pain and be able to do my work. I am 82 years old. I only take the tablets as I need them. Some times only one a day. I have no bad side effects as with aspirin or pain relievers. So I am all for you and your good work. May God bless you. I am on my last bottle of "Earth's Magic" now and am ordering some more.

Thanks Sincerely,
W. Kind
Kansas

Dear Sirs,
This is to let you know that I have been taking "Earth's Magic" for at least six months and it has helped me feel better. I have had not one side effect whatsoever. It helps my arthritis pain. I do hope I can continue to purchase this good product.

Mrs. M. Raman
Connecticut

Dear Sir,
I want to place another order for more "Earth's Magic" food tablets. Also I want to tell you how much good I think they did me. I have had my right knee joint replaced from arthritis. My left knee needs one, but I am trying to get by without it. So I've been taking

pain pills such as motrin and feldene, but they just keep my stomach upset. I have to buy medicine for my stomach. So this seems to relieve the pain and swelling without upsetting my stomach and for that I am grateful.

Sincerely,
Mrs. S. Chitwood
Arkansas

━━━━━━━━━━

Dear Mr. Anderson,

I appreciate your dedication in helping people who suffer with arthritis.

I have taken your product for six years-APRH and Earth's Magic, and believe they are totally natural and healthy. I have gone through two pregnancies during this time and these herbs were the only form of medication I could take that would not harm my babies and yet give me relief from the pain and stiffness of rheumatoid arthritis.

I commend you on your struggles of trying to keep Earth's Magic on the market for us.

God Bless,
D. Jorgensen
Montana

Dear Mr. Anderson,
I would like you to know the great improvement my husband and I have had since we have been using your product "Earth's Magic Herbs." The magic is no side effects, and we feel 15 years younger.

We feel the courts should weigh in favor of the user to prevent unnecessary suffering.

Thank-you,
K.J. Dyas
Washington

P.S. God Bless You

Mr. R.J. Anderson of Earth's Magic,

I sure hope you get this all straightened out with the F.D.A. I don't know what I'd do without my Earth's Magic tablets. I started on them over a year ago at which time I couldn't hardly walk at all.

I was on medication that wasn't doing a thing for me. I took Earth's Magic in to my doctors and both of them OK'd it for me. I was able to stop one of the drugs I was on and my children could tell a difference right away in the way I was getting around. Do hope you will get this all straightened out before too long. I'm lucky as I just had gotten a big order from you so I will be OK for a few months. Lots of luck.

D. Silva
California

Executive Office
The White House
1600 Pennsylvania Avenue
Washington, D.C. 20500

Dear President of the United States:

We the people, citizens of these great UNITED STATES of AMERICA, in order to provide justice for all hereby demand:

That we be informed truthfully, the information regarding EARTH'S MAGIC.

We, as citizens, demand the right of free choice. We are an educated, intelligent society.

We will choose of our own free will whether or not we wish to use the product, but our right to be informed cannot be denied!

Thank you,

_____

_____

_____

Zip code _____